THEATRICAL MAKEUP

THEATRICAL MAKEUP

Bert Broe

Consultant makeup artist

Pelham Books

First published in Great Britain by
Pelham Books Ltd
44 Bedford Square, London WC1B 3DU
1984

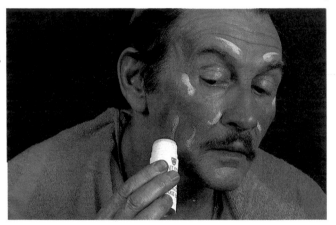

British Library Cataloguing
in Publication Data

Theatrical Makeup
1. Make-up, Theatrical
792′.027   PN2068

ISBN 0-7207-1526-1

Edited, designed and produced
by Spectator Publications
Photography by Michael Cyprien
Research Miranda Smith

Filmset in Rockwell by
BAS Printers Limited
Over Wallop, Stockbridge
Hampshire SO20 8JD
Photographs originated by
Fotographics Limited
44 Uxbridge Street, London W8 7TG
Printed and bound by
Mateu Cromo, Artes Graficas,
Madrid, Spain

Contents

Foreword

Somewhere beneath every Count Dracula or Frankenstein's Monster there is an ordinary actor doing a night's work. Picture them without makeup (a fangless Dracula, a chinless monster) or take a look at the very first photographs in this book. These show me as King Lear, progressively stripped of my makeup. Try to imagine the last bare-faced version on the heath, raging at the storm. Without the wild hair and ragged beard, poor Lear has to shout even louder to get his message across.

Looking back on a career of some forty years in the theatre, I realize it would have been totally impossible for me to have attempted seventy per cent of the parts I have played on stage without the use of make-up.

You would think therefore that one of the most important classes in any drama school would be concerned with make-up. Yet time and time again one meets young actors with every conceivable drama-school award, and with little or no knowledge of make-up.

Of course, these days, in films and television there is so much type-casting that make-up is used less and less, but on stage and especially in the classics, it is still of paramount importance. (I don't know too many actors who could play, say, Caliban, without make-up!)

When I played John Aubrey in *Brief Lives* for over one thousand seven hundred performances around the world, the make-up took just over three hours. (A somewhat daunting task when the end result could be a school's matinée in Hobart!) Friends who saw the show often asked if such a long process was necessary. "Surely," they would say, "if you just use a pale base, put on the wig, the beard and false nose, it would look the same from the stalls?!"

Perhaps they were right; perhaps it was an indulgence on my part; but you see, that whole period of making-up was my preparation for assuming the character. My dresser often said for the last thirty minutes before "curtain up" I would begin to speak in John Aubrey's voice. However, more important for me was the image I saw in my mirror before I went on stage. It had to be convincing – to me. It had to look like a genuine old man and not like an aerial view of Clapham Junction, for that final image I saw in the mirror before going on stage for $2\frac{1}{2}$ hours was the image I carried in my mind's eye and if I had not been convinced it was John Aubrey I could not have

sustained such a lengthy monologue.

I recommend this book highly because, in my opinion, it contains, in the simplest terms, all that is necessary to give the actor (amateur or professional), a thorough, comprehensive grounding in the art of stage makeup from which he can take-off and conduct his own experiments, gain practical experience, and, of course, greatly increase his range as an actor.

Mr Bert Broe, the artist responsible for the 'paintings' in this book has a simple, direct approach to the subject which makes it appear interesting and easy – which, indeed, it is.

Roy Dotrice

Introduction

All actors, amateur and professional, must develop a wide range of skills before they become equipped to give convincing performances on stage. They must learn to stand, walk, talk and even think in chararacter. They must take on their new identity in order to become part of a most elaborately contrived deception whose aim is to engage and entertain an audience for a matter of hours or so.

This book is concerned with just one important aspect of the actor's craft, theatrical makeup. Most of you will do you own makeup, the lucky ones having been briefed by a professional makeup artist at rehearsal and perhaps even for the first one or two actual performances. Whether you enjoy that benefit or not, you must understand *why* you are making up before you can hope to do it with any great distinction.

This book has been devised to help the amateur actor who wants to achieve professional standards of theatrical makeup. Our makeup expert, Bert Broe, has spent twenty years lecturing and giving advice on all forms of theatrical makeup to both professional and amateur actors, and in this book he passes on to you the benefit of his vast experience so that your performances can profit from first-class makeup.

Whilst effective makeup must be objective, the most brilliant work will not save a bad play or a poor actor, but intelligent, sensitive and thoughtful makeup can play a most important supporting role, among an ingenious set, skilful lighting, imaginative costume and inspired direction, in the creation of successful theatrical productions of all sorts.

But why use makeup at all? The main aim, of course, is to help an actor or actress assume the physical and emotional characteristics of the part they are playing. Sometimes dramatists and writers give clear indications on how they see their characters. Sometimes a director, or a group of actors working together, may have a particular view of how a play should look, perhaps moving it backwards or forwards in time or shifting its setting by thousands of miles. Here again, effective use of makeup can be vital.

What makes successful makeup? Preparation, planning and forethought are the first essentials. You will not do yourself justice if you arrive shortly before you are due to go on, and then try to transform yourself in five minutes. The length of time needed to make yourself up will depend upon how complicated and demanding are the requirements of the part, and on your own skill and experience, but you should allow a minimum of twenty minutes for a makeup of average complexity, and ensure yourself plenty of time for practice before your first night appearance!

Makeup rehearsals should start with lighting rehearsals, not at the dress-rehearsal. Indeed, to find exactly the right balance between your makeup and the stage lighting so that as many of the audience as possible can see you and become completely involved with your portrayal is as important as achieving the right effect for the size and shape of your theatre. Do not be deceived by your dressing-room mirror. Remember that one of the audience straining to see you from the back of the stalls, or from the gallery, will need much more help, that is a heavier makeup than you think he may need as you gaze into your looking-glass no more than an arm's length away.

In the chapters that follow, we shall be illustrating these points and many others in this practical and comprehensive guide to a wide range of makeup techniques and applications. You will find advice to help you choose your basic makeup kit, and how to use greasepaint and water-soluble colours. We shall tell you about "Straight" and "Corrective" makeups. We explore the exotic makeup used in pantomime with graphic demonstrations of how to make yourself into a convincing fairy, pantomime dame or devil.

People, in real life and in the make-believe world of the theatre, come in all shapes and sizes, and is there anything more disparate than human personality? This book will show you how to achieve convincing transformations, how to age yourself by thirty years within the span of a two-hour performance, and how to change from a slim, healthy appearance to a gross, dissipated hulk; how to become a god or a queen, a vicar or a tart.

You will discover how to convey, through the art of a stage makeup, a wide range of personality traits from deceit and cunning to kindness and generosity, and with this detailed guidance we list four hundred celebrated dramatic characters of widely varying personality, so that you will be able to select the particular combination of attributes to suit the role you are to play.

Bert Broe has two generations of theatrical wigmakers and makeup artists behind him. The family's first involvement with the world of theatre began when his grandfather, Bert, was apprenticed to and ultimately manager of Clarkson's, the famous costumiers and wigmakers, at the turn of the century. After a few years and much hard work, he left to set up his own business in Paddington, under the name of 'Bert', a name which was to become famous in the 1920's as "Wigs by 'Bert'" appeared on theatre programmes throughout the land. Helped by his son, Bert Broe's father, the business expanded and over the next 30 years was supplying wigs and makeup to the famous actors of the time through Lillian Bayliss at the Old Vic and Sadler's Wells. The family did not associate themselves only with the rich and famous, however: their busy schedule included school plays and amateur dramatic productions, hospital and company shows countrywide.

In the late 1940's, Bert Broe began work for his father full time, having accompanied him as a child to shows across the country. He became briefly involved in the film industry as a studio wigmaker and although other members of the family found a home in the film industry, Bert's first allegience remained to the theatre, to which he returned in the 1950's. Since then he has made his father's crafts his own, developing his skills as makeup artist as well as wigmaker.

Determined to see many would-be actors off to a good start, Bert Broe began lecturing in makeup techniques at drama school in London in the 1960's, and now holds the posts of lecturer at a number of Great Britain's top drama and opera schools. Together with his wife, Pamela, Bert owns and runs a successful shop in Covent Garden, London, called "The Theatre-Zoo" which supplies a comprehensive range of theatrical costumes and makeup to both professional and amateur markets.

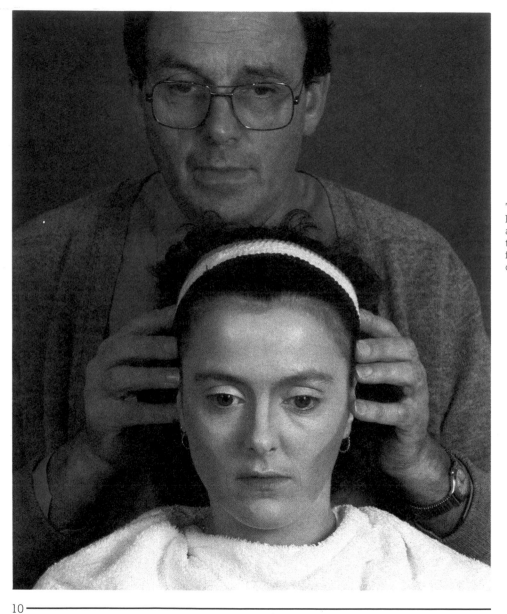

Two current generations of the Broe family seen here as Bert and his daughter Jane work together to produce the makeup for the series of photographs on pages 34 and 35

Tools of the Trade

An actor's appearance on stage is every bit as important as what he says and does. Yet he needs very little basic equipment to make his face a portrait of the character he is playing. The components of a basic makeup kit are shown and described in this chapter. It is not necessary to buy a wide range of materials at the start; apart from the considerable expense, you would probably use few of them regularly. It is worth bearing in mind, too, that although more than a hundred different makeup colours are available commercially, you can achieve most of them yourself simply by mixing from quite a limited palette of colours, and you can always add to your kit when you need to.

Be prepared to invest in the basic equipment recommended here. You must have a kit of your own; relying upon other people's makeup is a good way to become unpopular.

Besides the makeup, you will need one or two towels or a cape to protect your clothes (especially if you are using spirit gum), a hairband to hold your hair away from your face, and a box of cottonwool or cleansing tissues for cleaning up. The kit that Bert Broe has devised for the beginner is comprehensive without being extravagant and comprises the following items:

Base makeup is the foundation which gives the skin the colour that is most suitable for the character you are playing and into which all the subsequently applied colours will be blended. Two types are available: greasepaint, which comes in stick form and is applied with the fingers, a brush or direct from the stick, and water-soluble, as a cake or a liquid, which is applied with a moist sponge or makeup brush.

Greasepaint is the traditional form of stage makeup and is, in many ways, easier to use than the water-soluble type. It reflects light in much the same way as skin does and, because it blends more easily than water-soluble, it can be used to achieve more subtle gradations of tone. It is also the more economical form of base makeup. Be careful in applying it, however. If your face is not thoroughly clean, or if you use it too heavily, you can become uncomfortably hot under the stage lights.

As a rule, you will need no more than five or six colours, of which you may use only two or three regularly, because a wide range of skin tones can be achieved by mixing a light colour, e.g. Leichner No. 3, 4½ or 5, with a darker colour, e.g. Leichner Nos 8 or 9. Leichner and Kryolan are two of the best-known brands. There is a very wide range of base colour greasepaint sticks available if you want to invest in them.

Water soluble base comes as Pan-Cake, as an opaque liquid and as a transparent liquid dye. The three types have one thing in common – they can all be removed by washing. Water-soluble base is more difficult to work with than greasepaint and can look masklike if too much of it is applied. However, it should always be used where the skin comes into contact with costumes – for example, under the chin – and for general body makeup. Greasepaint rubs off easily onto costumes, from which it is difficult to remove.

Because water-based makeup is not easy to blend, more colours will be needed to achieve the same wide range of effects that are possible with the number of greasepaint sticks listed in the previous section.

For body makeup, you can use the water soluble makeups recommended in the basic makeup kit opposite, but Leichner Eau-de-Lys, Kryolan Wet Makeup or the impermanent dye, Kryolan Body Tint, are less expensive.

Leichner and Kryolan greasepaint colours are referred to by number – for example L (Leichner) No. 7 and K (Kryolan) No. 512.

Lining colours are stronger than base colours, and come in narrow sticks called "liners", and in palettes. Both greasepaint and water-soluble forms are available. They are applied either direct from the stick or with a fine brush, and are used to emphasize shadows and highlights, skin creases and wrinkles. They are also used for eyes and lips. In general, you will need no more than six to eight greasepaint colours, because a wide range of shades can be obtained by mixing, as with the base colours. Include Crimson Lake, Medium Blue, Black, White, Carmine and Coffee Brown in your kit.

The liners and palette colours are simply referred to by colour – for example, Crimson Lake and Coffee Brown.

Makeup pencils, these wax pencils are used to outline the eyes, to accentuate the eyebrows, to outline the lips and to shade wrinkles. They are made in several colours, but only Brown and Black are really necessary for your basic kit.

A special tool is sold for sharpening makeup pencils because ordinary sharpeners would tear the soft wax, and get blocked with the trimmings.

Brushes and sponges, brushes made of sable hair are best for applying lining colours. The bristles of theatre makeup brushes are short and dense, making them firm and therefore easy to control. You will probably need no more than two – a No. 2, which has bristles ⅛ inch wide, and a No. 6, which has bristles ¼ inch wide.

A sponge, synthetic or natural, is essential if you are using water-soluble makeup. Plastic stipple sponges are useful for creating the impression of

Basic Makeup Kit

Greasepaint:
Leichner base colours
for women
- No. 3 (Medium Pink)
- No. 5 (Ivory)
- No. 6 (Sallow Pink)
- No. 7 (Coffee Brown)
- No. 9 (Brick Red)

for men
- No. 3½ (Light Tan)
- No. 5 (Ivory)
- No. 6 (Sallow Pink)
- No. 7 (Coffee Brown)
- No. 8 (Golden Tan)

or Kryolan paintsticks of
equivalent colours

Kryolan TZ palette
containing the following
greasepaint colours:

Black (42)	Medium Blue
White (20)	(326M)
Crimson Lake	Carmine 2
(25)	Coffee Brown (7)

or Leichner liners of equivalent
colours

Water-soluble makeup;
Max Factor PanCakes
for women
- Natural
- Tan 1
- 24 or 25
- Light Egyptian (for shading)
- White (for highlighting)

for men
- Tan 2
- 26 or 27
- Light Egyptian (for shading)
- White (for highlighting)

or Kryolan Aquacolours

for women	*for men*
F2	O14
3W or 4W	5W or 7W
OA (Old Age)	OA (Old Age)

Kryolan TZ palette
containing the following
water-soluble colours:

Black (42)	Medium Blue
White (20)	(326M)
Crimson Lake	Carmine 2
(25)	Coffee Brown (7)

Basic Makeup Kit
continued

Cantilever makeup box
Sponge
Makeup brushes,
   Nos 2 and 6
Wax pencils,
   Black and Brown
Mascara (for women),
   Black and Brown
Wax pencil sharpener
Powder – Leichner Neutral
   or Kryolan TL2 or 3

Powder puff
Powder brush
Stipple sponge
Removing cream
   or Kryolan Hydra
Tissues
Cottonwool
Towels
Hairband or hairnet
Blunt-ended scissors
Tail-comb

skin textures and for introducing irregularities into a foundation. Special squirrel hair brushes are made for the removal of surplus powder.

Powder, applied with a puff, is used to 'fix' or set the makeup. Use neutral or translucent face powder so as not to alter the colour of your makeup, and remove the excess with a squirrel hair brush. To help with certain special effects, a pure white powder is available (see page 43).

Removing agents, in addition to the proprietary brands available at theatrical stockists, most types of cleansing cream sold by chemists will remove greasepaint. There is also an oil, Kryolan Hydra, which is rubbed into the makeup and then washed off. Water-soluble colour can be washed off with soap and water.

Makeup box, acquire a cantilever box or a box fitted with loose trays, preferably a lockable one. Never leave it where the makeup can get hot – by the back window of a car or on a radiator.

Special Makeup

A wide range of products exists to create special effects. Such items are not essential for the amateur to begin with, but they can usefully form part of a larger kit. They include nose putty, derma wax, old-skin plastic, bloods, tooth enamels, bald caps, wigs, hairpieces, hair sprays and Eyebrow Plastic.

Nose putty and derma wax, you can give yourself a Roman nose or a fiercely determined chin with these materials. They can also be used to simulate wounds, scars and skin blemishes. Both materials are self-adhesive, but the wax is more malleable, and suitable for subtle modelling, like bags under the eyes (see page 65).

Old-skin plastic, collodion and Tuplast are liquid plastics that are painted on the skin for special effects, they all contract as they dry. The wrinkles created by old-skin plastic are very realistic, but to use it effectively requires a great deal of experience. You can use collodion or Tuplast as an alternative to putty or wax, to create scars.

Crêpe hair, if you do not have time, do not want to, or cannot grow a beard or moustache, then you can make them with crêpe hair. Made of wool, it comes in tightly-woven braids in most of the natural hair colours. It can be used crimped, or it may be straightened. It is stuck on to the face with spirit gum, and removed with the aid of a spirit gum solvent (see page 62–63).

Hairpieces are either machine-made with man-made fibre, or of real hair. You can hire or buy wigs, switches, falls, curls, chignons, toupées and back pieces. You can buy beards and moustaches only from specialist shops. If you are hiring, you must never wash, cut or attempt to restyle the hairpiece. If you are buying, always follow the manufacturer's cleaning instructions. Use only spirit gum to fix hairpieces in position; rubber adhesive is nearly impossible to remove.

Bald caps, there are two kinds of bald caps available – expensive and less expensive! The less expensive ones are strong but thick, so the edges do not mould well to the head and you will need to do a lot of work with makeup to disguise the join. The other kind, the expensive ones, are so thin as to be virtually undetectable, but they are likely to tear when they are taken off (see pages 66–67).

Spirit gum, this liquid adhesive is used to fix crêpe hair, wigs, hairpieces and bald caps. Different makes of spirit gum take different lengths of time to dry, but they all dry quickly. A solvent is sold for removing spirit gum but always wash your face thoroughly afterwards; spirit gum and the solvent can irritate some skins.

Hair sprays, use lacqueur spray to hold hair in place if you are creating a special style with your hair. To tint hair, you can buy colour and glitter sprays in several shades. Comb the sprays in as they dry and remove them by washing. Whenever you are using sprays of any sort, be careful to shield your eyes – you can do this with a free hand or with a card or paper pattern cut to the hairline.

There is a danger with dyed, bleached, naturally blonde or white hair that the colours may stain. Lacquering the hair before spraying it with colour will reduce the risk, but there is no certain method of prevention.

Eyebrow Plastic comes in stick form and is used to cover up eyebrows; you simply press it on. To remove, soften the plastic with cleansing cream and then wipe it off.

An alternative method of hiding the eyebrows is to apply moistened bar soap. Use just enough soap to smooth down the hairs. But do not use bar soap if you are likely to perspire heavily or you will end up with an eyeful of salty, soapy water. To remove it, wipe the soap off with cottonwool soaked in water. Do this separately from the removal of any other makeup.

Bloods Be wary of theatrical blood; it can stain costumes. Of the two makes of liquid 'blood' available, Leichner Casualty Simulation and Kryolan Special Film Blood are recommended. The former is dark red. Special Film Blood is available in two colours, light and dark; your choice will depend upon the nature of the stage lighting. It is runnier than the Leichner product, but both are realistic, viscous liquids.

Supplementary Materials

Nose putty, Naturo Plasto
   or Kryolan Special Wax
Sealor
Collodion or Tuplast
Old-skin plastic
Crêpe hair
Wigs
Hairpieces
Toothbrush
Bald cap(s)
Spirit gum
M.M.E. Kryolan
   spirit gum solvent
Rouge
Eyebrow Plastic
   or bar soap
Leichner Casualty
   Simulation or Kryolan
   Special Film Blood
Coloured wax pencils,
   a variety of colours
   are available
White powder,
   Kryolan TL (Translucent) l
Hairsprays,
   lacquer, colour, glitter
Tooth enamels
Fixier Spray

There are also gelatin capsules containing powder or crystals which turn to 'blood' when crushed in the mouth. Leichner Blood Capsules effervesce while the Kryolan equivalent do not. You should practise using the capsules, as the timing can be critical. Allow a few seconds for their contents to mix with the saliva before attempting to let the 'blood' trickle out of your mouth.

'Blood' sachets which burst under pressure are useful for stage fights. These are not available commercially, but you can make them easily enough. Soak a sponge in liquid 'blood' and wrap it in cling-film. Under pressure, the cling-film will separate, and the 'blood' will seep out.

Kryolan Fix Blood is a gel which stays glossy even when dry, so that it continues to look like wet blood. It peels off easily, but has the disadvantage of being rather expensive.

You can hire knives which dribble 'blood' when the hilt is squeezed!

Tooth enamels come in three colours – Black, Nicotine and White. They are easy to apply to dry teeth, but may need touching up during a long performance. The white tooth enamel is brilliant and sometimes shows up too much against other teeth. Remove enamels with a toothbrush or by scraping them off with a fingernail.

The Dressing-room

You may find yourself making up in a dressing-room which is luxurious and well-equipped, or in a sectioned-off area at the back of a village hall. Whatever the circumstances, there are certain pieces of equipment that you will need and conditions under which you should aim to work if you are to make up properly:

A working surface and chair, be comfortably seated and ensure that the working surface is large enough for you to be able to spread out all of your materials. It is vital that there is plenty of room around the table so that you are not jostled whilst doing any one of the many jobs which demand a steady hand and a delicate touch.

Lay your colours out in the same order each time, as an artist would lay his colours out on a palette. You will find it easier and quicker to use the makeup if you have it all in front of you. Do not tidy away unnecessarily whilst working with your makeup – wait until you have finished before putting away your materials and cleaning up the working surface for the next performance.

A mirror, which should be large enough for you to see all of the parts you need to work on, so that you can sit comfortably while lacquering your Marie Antoinette wig or sticking on a hairy caveman's chest. The mirror should be well lit by tungsten lighting, never make up under neon lighting. You cannot match the intensity and colour temperature of stage lighting in the dressing room, but you should be aware of the effect that it will have. It may worry you that your makeup appears clumsy seen in the mirror, but experience will teach you to judge exactly the effect it will have on the more distant audience.

A water source, a good dressing-room will have a wash-basin. If this is not the case, there should at least be a water source nearby and you could perhaps keep a water container in the dressing-room. If you are using water-soluble makeup, you must have a bowl of clean water to work with.

Good ventilation is very necessary, particularly if you are using volatile materials like aerosols and solvents.

Theory and Application

When you make up for the stage, you are painting a character on a living canvas. That character will be convincing only if you are thoroughly acquainted with your own face, and aware of the effects that stage lighting and distance from the audience will have upon it.

Facial Structure

Before you begin to make up, sit in front of a mirror and look carefully at your face. Feel for the bone structure: the brow, the cheekbones, the jawbone.

You can alter the appearance of the face with makeup, but you can work only within the frame that is there. When you have understood where the bones of the face lie, you will be able to play with the effects of light and shade so as to enhance your features or to create a new character.

The Texture of the Skin

The texture of your skin may dictate whether to use water-soluble or greasepaint makeup. For example, if you have open-pored skin, you are likely to perspire heavily and in that case, greasepaint might be more suitable for you because the sweat will not leave trail-marks on it.

The Colour of the Skin

For a straight makeup (see pages 22–25) the choice of base colour should be founded on your natural complexion and should compensate for the bleaching effect that stage lighting and distance from the audience will cause. On rare occasions, when you are working close to the audience or are acting in daylight, there will be no need to use foundation makeup. Shading and highlighting alone should be sufficient to achieve the desired effect.

For a character makeup, you may well need to choose a base colour that is a very different colour from your own complexion, but you must still bear in mind the bleaching effect of the stage lighting.

Expression

The bone structure of the face is immobile. Expression comes from the use of a complex set of facial muscles, and the way in which these move and cause the fleshy parts of the face to move. Whether you are enhancing existing features or creating a completely new character, you must discover how your face works.

The most important of the features that convey expression are the eyes and the mouth. Particular consideration must be given to these when you are deciding how to make yourself up.

Shadows and Highlights

Like any solid object, the face reveals its form by the juxtaposition of light and shadow. The art of the makeup artist lies in knowing and understanding the "topography" of the face.

Stand directly under a light and look at yourself in a mirror. The depressions will be in shadow – the temples, the eye-sockets, either side of the nose, underneath the cheekbones and above the point of the chin. Note also the lines on your face – each one is the deepest part of a shadow.

The overhead light will brighten certain areas on your face – the forehead, the bridge of the nose, the ridge of the jaw and the chin itself. If you wish to reinforce these features, you will need to apply a lighter colour, known as a highlight, to them. The addition of a highlight beside a dark line will add depth and form to the latter.

Stage Lighting

Inexperienced performers will have little or no idea of how they appear to an audience under lights. Sit in at a rehearsal and observe the lighting and the way in which it affects the players' makeup. Always check with the Director or Producer that your makeup is effective from the auditorium; if neither is available, ask someone, on whose judgement you can rely, for their opinion. There are very few productions today in which footlights are used. All the lighting comes from above, from the wings and from front-of-house. Its intensity dictates the strength of the makeup you should use. The brighter the lights, the paler you will appear on stage. The colour of the stage lighting will influence the colours you use because it determines how the audience sees those colours. It can affect makeup to the point of making it seem to fade, darken and even change colour completely. Always be alive to any changes, however subtle, that the Director decides to make to the lighting-plot, and be ready to adjust your makeup if necessary.

Distance

Today's audiences do not want to be aware of makeup and the more intimate the production, the less you should use. If you are working very close to them, for example on the stage of a 'theatre-in-the-round', rely more on the highlights than on the shadows. The tone of a shadow can become very obtrusive at close range.

If you are working in a traditional theatre, then of course you should not make up only for the front rows of the stalls. Be aware that the audience at the back of the gallery must also be able to see you, preferably without those plastic binoculars!

The Application of Makeup

Applying the base makeup

Before applying any makeup, clean your face thoroughly. Remove any existing makeup with cleansing cream and then by washing. Make sure that any excess oil or grease is removed; an oily face is difficult to work on. There is no need for men to shave immediately before making up because the base makeup will mask a normal beard shadow. Always use a hairband or hairnet to hold back the hair from the face. Ensure that clothing which needs to go over the head is put on or taken off before you begin to make up, and cover the shoulders and lap with towels for protection.

You can carry a wide range of base colours, or you can mix many of them from the small range of selected colours recommended in the basic makeup kit on page 13. The beginner would be well advised to use a hand as a palette for mixing. The more experienced actor will mix the colours direct on the face.

Apply the base makeup to the cheeks close to the sides of the nose, and to the centre of the forehead, and work it outwards evenly. Greasepaint can be applied direct from the stick, with the fingers or with a brush, but water-soluble materials must be spread from a damp sponge or brush. Put on an opaque layer, but only just enough to mask your complexion; too much greasepaint will quickly become sticky and unmanageable.

If you overdo one colour when mixing several on the face, you will have to compensate with another; that will result in there being too much makeup on the face. You can always add more if you have put on too little. Just as you need to make up your face, remember to make up any other part of your body which is exposed and, in order to protect your clothing, use water-soluble makeup for this purpose.

Shading and Highlighting

Shadow and highlight colours are normally applied on top of the base makeup. There are, however, some occasions when, to achieve a special effect, you will apply some shading or highlighting before the base, for example to rejuvenate the face (see pages 32–33).

When shading and highlighting, apply the dark, shadow colours first, and then the highlights to those areas that catch the light. Put colour in the darkest part of a shadow or the lightest part of a highlight and blend it outwards.

The direction of any shadow you are putting on the face is important. For example, one of the methods used to thin the face is to apply shading beneath the cheekbone, shaping it in towards the nose (see page 34). This accentuates the shape of the bone structure and gives a thin and gaunt appearance. If you want to look fatter, shadows and highlights must be used to emphasize the fleshier parts of the face (see pages 36–37).

Blending

Blending is the business of smoothing darker or lighter colours into the base colour evenly so that there are no hard edges. Tones rarely go suddenly from light to dark, they are usually gradated. If you want a strong makeup with contrast, you must reduce the tonal range; if you want a softer one, you increase it. Where there is an abrupt change of plane – for example on the cheekbone – the gradation will be more sudden than on a gentler curve.

Greasepaint colours blend easily on a greasepaint base and even at the darkest part of the shadow, there will be a mixture of colours. With water-soluble makeup on the other hand, the merging of colours can only be achieved by breaking them down where they meet, with a wet brush – you literally paint one colour into another. Some experienced actors choose to use greasepaint and water-soluble materials in combination. If you eventually decide that you prefer this technique, put on the greasepaint first, as the two will blend more easily.

Powdering

Powdering sets the makeup and should be applied generously with a puff. Use a soft brush to remove the excess. For most makeups you will use flesh coloured powder, but for special effects, white powder is also available (see page 43).

Eyebrows and eyelashes

The finishing task with any makeup is to touch in the eyebrows with an eyebrow pencil. But before this, you should clean the eyelashes with a wet finger, wiping off any makeup that may have gathered there.

If you want to change the shape of your eyebrows, flatten the hairs by working Eyebrow Plastic or moistened bar soap into them, before applying makeup to the face. The soap will need time to dry, but you can work over Eyebrow Plastic immediately because it is not wet. Cover the parts of the eyebrows you have treated in this way with base makeup and, after powdering, draw in the new shape.

Teeth

The whole character of the mouth can be considerably changed by the appearance of the teeth. If they need to be broken down or blacked out altogether, use tooth enamel, simply painting it on. If can be removed with a toothbrush or a fingernail. Be thoughtful in your use of tooth enamel – most people's teeth are not pure white, and so white enamel can look very odd and unnatural.

Throughout the captions in this book, the trade names Leichner and Kryolan have been abbreviated to L and K respectively.

Straight Makeup – Male

The aim of Straight Makeup is to put on just the right strength of colour to compensate for bright stage lighting and for the loss of definition caused by the distance between actor and audience. Straight makeup does not involve any alteration to the features, or any suggestion of a character other than your own. Therefore, in choosing which colours to use, bear in mind the natural colour of your skin, the type of stage lighting and the size of the theatre. The brighter the lights and the greater the distance from the audience, the stronger the colour. You will need to experiment until you achieve the right effect.

Above Study your complexion to decide upon the most appropriate base colour
Right above Cover your face with enough base to just mask out your own colouring
Right below Shape the cheekbones with L No. 8
Far right above Always draw in the bottom eyeline first
Far right centre Now use the black eyeliner to outline the top lash
Far right below Colour the lips with L No. 8

Remember always to clean your face thoroughly before making up. Tie back your hair and spread towels on your shoulders and lap to protect your clothing.

This makeup establishes a standard procedure: apply the base, restore the beard shadow that has been covered by the base; shade the cheeks; draw in eyelines; colour the lips, making them darker than the base; powder; clean the eyelashes and clean and define the eyebrows; and, finally, make up the neck with Aquacolour. These pictures show the use of greasepaint, and eyeliner and a brush.

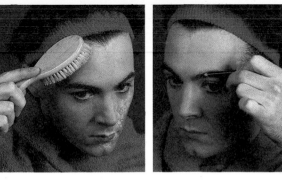

Left Drench the makeup with translucent powder
Far left below Remove surplus powder with a soft brush
Left below Define the eyebrows with your black or brown pencil
Above Always remember to make up your neck and ears and any other exposed parts of your body – with Aquacolour K TV7 in this case

Straight Makeup – Female

Straight makeup for a woman is only very subtly different from that for a man: apply the base, shade the cheeks, use colour on the eyelids; draw in eyelines; apply Carmine or Crimson Lake to the lips; powder; define the eyebrows; clean the eyelashes and apply mascara; and, finally, make up the neck with Aquacolour.

The use of water-soluble makeup is shown here. Unlike greasepaint, which can be applied direct from the stick, on a finger or with a brush, water-soluble makeup must be applied with a dampened sponge or brush. Use it sparingly.

The amount of colour on the eyelids will depend largely upon fashion and the period in which the play is set. These factors will also influence the strength of shading on the cheekbones and the colour of the lips. The use of mascara in Straight makeup is strictly reserved for women.

Below left Use Carmine from the K TZ Aquacolour palette to shade under the cheekbones. *Below right* When applying the eyeshadow with a No. 6 brush, shade heavily on the eyelid

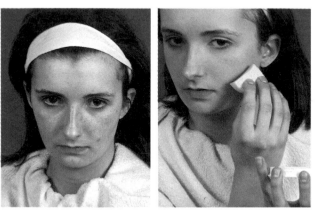

Above left Ready to start: clean face, hair held back and towel on to protect clothes. *Above right* Starting at the centre of the face, smooth on K F2 Aquacolour with a sponge

Above With an eyebrow pencil close to the lashes, draw lines along first the lower and then the upper lid. Colour the lips with K TZ Carmine (L No. 8 for men)

Left Apply translucent powder liberally over the whole of the face with a puff, and remove the excess with a soft brush

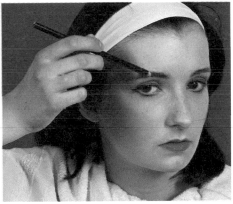

Above Touch in the eyebrows with an eyebrow pencil. Clear makeup and powder from the eyelashes and apply mascara

Corrective Makeup

Corrective makeup is designed to conceal irregularities or 'faults' in your natural appearance that might otherwise stand in the way of your stage role. It may mean changing the size of one eye, altering the shape of the nose, or even taping back a pair of flapping ears.

Think before doing corrective work. What you may think of as a fault in your face may actually be a strength on stage. An interesting face need not be a pretty one. Think twice before 'improving' it.

If, however, you and the Director are agreed that something does need changing, most corrections can be made with shadow and highlight. Shading near the hairline can make the forehead less high, or highlighting the centre of the nose more broadly than normal can make it seem wider. Shading of the jawline can make the chin seem more pointed; a deep shadow in the inner corners of the eyes will make them appear more sunken.

Blemishes Spots, scars, birth-marks and discolouration of the skin can all be covered by Kryolan Derma Colour or Innoxa Kermask, which are available in specialist shops. Alternatively, any discoloured area can be disguised with a water-based colour, lighter than the intended greasepaint base.

Eyes Most of us have eyes of slightly different sizes, but sometimes this becomes obtrusive. If there is a marked difference, emphasize the smaller eye with eye-liner. Never try to make the large eye look smaller. Dark colours on the eyelids will make the eyes appear to sink back into their sockets, while light colours here will bring the highlighted area forward.

Eyebrows Use Eyebrow Plastic or moistened bar soap to flatten the hairs before blocking out with base colour and establishing a new shape or less bushy eyebrows with an eyebrow pencil.

Mouth To make a small mouth larger, extend the corners with lip colour. To thin the lips, cover them with the base makeup and then draw in their new, reduced shape.

Nose You can use putty or wax to enlarge a nose (see page 65). Shade the sides of the nose to make it thinner (see page 34). A broad highlight down the centre will widen it, while a thin highlight will make it appear to be sharper. Extend a highlight across the bridge of the nose for a leonine brow.

Ears If your ears stick out, follow the example of the young Bing Crosby and use spirit gum or doublesided toupée tape to hold them back against the head. However, there is always a risk that any adhesive will not hold for long enough, and that the ears may spring back into their natural prominence during the performance!

Forehead To make the forehead appear less high, or narrower, strengthen the natural hairline with eyebrow pencil. Re-shape and raise the hairline with Eyebrow Plastic or bar soap, followed by base makeup. Alternatively, use a bald cap (see pages 66–67) with a wig, or a high hairline wig.

Jaw Apply shadow to the sides of the jawline to reduce the weight of a lantern jaw. Shade under the bone to make the jawline appear more substantial. You can use putty or wax for major alterations.

Character makeup is anything that is not Straight or Corrective makeup. Any change, however slight, to the actor's age, health, demeanour or view of life constitutes a change of character, and the makeup must reflect this. You may be ageing by only five years, or gaining a few pounds in weight, but you are creating a new character.

Long before you open your makeup box, there are things to be done. First, read the play. Many plays have detailed cast-lists which describe the characters. Or there may be a short character analysis in the Stage Directions for the actors' first entrances. You may glean important information from the comments characters make about each other, or about themselves. Sometimes the names will influence the makeup – Sir Andrew Aguecheek and Sir Toby Belch almost speak for themselves!

Second, consult your Director or Producer. Ideally, they will produce their own cast-list with a description of each character, giving age, background, physical characteristics, temperament etc. If a cast-list is not forthcoming, it is even more essential for you to consult your Director or Producer. Their interpretation of the characters is vital, and if you know what they are thinking, you may save yourself time and effort. It would be nonsense to make up Shylock as the archetypal mean and nasty Jew if – as sometimes happens – the Director intends to portray him as representing a persecuted minority.

Consider the character you have now discovered. How do you picture him or her? Think of his skin colour; is he young or old? An outdoor or an indoor person? Consider the form of his face; has he particularly wide eyes or a long nose? A plan of action is necessary if you are to achieve a convincing character makeup, and you should have a mental image of how the finished result will appear to the audience.

If you find it difficult to imagine the character, then either you or the Director should put pen to paper and sketch the image. You can get a lot of ideas simply by observing people around you, while for historical productions, books and old magazines provide useful reference.

Now, with this imaginary character in your mind's eye, consider your own face. Unless, by some extraordinary coincidence, you do already resemble the person you are about to portray on stage, you must decide how best to alter or adapt your own features.

Forehead

Shading can radically alter the shape of the forehead. Heavy shadows at the temples emphasize the skull and give a gaunt, emaciated look that is appropriate to either a very old or very thin character. Shading along the hairline and at the temples can make the forehead seem less prominent than it is naturally. To lengthen the forehead, the hairline can be raised with a high hairline wig. If you use a bald cap or high hairline wig, carry any lines on the forehead across the edge of the wig.

Age, grief and anger all create lines. Where they are in character, use existing lines; any additional ones must not be in conflict with the natural movements of the face.

Eyes

Eye makeup is especially important in creating a stage character. Highlights and eyeshadow can make the eyes look larger or smaller. A heavy eyeline on the rim of the top lash will make them seem larger. To make them look smaller, do not extend the top eyeline beyond the outside corner of the eye and begin the bottom eyeline close to the inner corner. Highlighting, rather than shading the eyelid will make the eye seem more prominent, heavy shading of the eyelid up to the eyebrow and deep shadow in the inner corner of the eye sinks it back into its socket. Highlights in the inner corners of the eyes, or a wide highlight on the bridge of the nose between the eyes, will make them seem farther apart than they already are.

Crow's feet, or laugh-lines, become more marked with age and add usefully to characterization. If these have been masked out by the base, you may need to reinstate them. Old age and ill-health can be suggested by red rims to the eyes; soft darkening under the eyes has the same effect. Heavier shading and bags under the yes are associated with insomnia, more acute infirmity and dissipation.

Eyebrows

Many expressions are conveyed by the eyebrows. Try looking quizzical without them! To change their shape, mask out the parts you wish to lose, with Eyebrow Plastic or bar soap, and apply the base more heavily to those areas than you do to the rest of the face. To add to eyebrows, either shade with an eyebrow pencil, or fill them out with crêpe hair. When shaping or touching in eyebrows, use short, light strokes of the pencil and always follow the direction of the hairs.

Like hair, eyebrows have been affected by changes in fashion through the ages. It is worth checking reference material for the appearance of eyebrows in whatever period your play is set. Eyebrows change with age. They tend to get more scruffy, so either comb them to make them look untidy or draw in hairs out of place. If you want to achieve an ageing effect more simply, you can grey the eyebrows with Kryolan palette White or White paintstick. Eyebrows are valuable features for an actor, and deserve your careful attention.

Cheeks

If your character's face needs some colour, then add a little Carmine or Crimson Lake to the base on the cheeks. If you need high colour, apply dry Rouge to the cheeks after powdering. Never try to shape or blend Rouge, simply apply it and leave it.

To make the cheekbones more prominent, highlight the high point of the bone itself, and shade beneath it. Young people seem to have high cheekbones, but they also become more prominent as a result of illness and old age. For round cheeks, shade outwards horizontally from the nostril, to give the impression of sagging flesh. Then highlight the new centre of the cheek.

Nose

Thin, sharp noses can convey the feeling of cunning or inquisitiveness. A wide red nose, suitably pockmarked, can imply dissipation and an over-fondness for the bottle.

Shading and highlighting will transform a nose. You can even give the impression (seen from the front) of a broken nose by drawing a wide, crooked highlight down the centre. A touch of colour inside the nostrils will flare them; shadows outside the nostrils will tend to counteract any natural flare. Shadows at the side of the nose, separated by a thin highlight will lengthen it. A highlight across the top of the bridge will shorten and thicken it. A broad highlight drawn right down the centre, will make a nose seem much wider.

Nose-Mouth Crease

The nose-mouth crease runs from the side of the nostril downwards, sometimes to join up with the corner of the mouth. It is present in most people in middle and old age, but is more noticeable in some than in others. For character makeup, it can be made vertical and elongated to thin the face. If it is curved outwards and slightly upwards at the bottom, it will frame and fill the cheeks.

Mouth

The choice of lip colouring depends on the state of health, age and sex of the character. Fashion should be taken into account – particularly with females. Old age and sickness often make the lips pale, thin and pinched.

The mouth can be made to look larger or fuller by altering the shape of the lips with colour. To make the lips thinner or to change their shape altogether, cover them with base makeup and paint in the new shape before powdering. If you are changing the shape of the lips, it helps to define their new shape by outlining with Crimson Lake on a No.2 brush, before filling in with your chosen lip colour.

With age, the muscles around the mouth relax, the skin sags and more lines appear. The teeth discolour and can decay. Create the lines with shading and highlighting, and use tooth enamel to block out the edges of the teeth and make them look jagged. Be careful when blocking out a tooth completely, the effect may be inadvertently comic.

Jawline and Neck

With obesity or age, sagging flesh around the jaw and neck creates jowls and double chins. Highlight existing loose flesh, or use shadows to suggest it. For a double chin, draw a band or shadow under the jaw. For a firmer, more youthful appearance, shade directly under the line of the jawbone. Then run a band of highlight along the line, softening its lower edge into the shadow colour, but leaving its upper edge virtually untouched.

Age shows in the neck as much as in the face. Be sure to create jowls and lines consistent with those that have been drawn on the face.

With character makeup, you can appear old or young, fat or thin, happy or morose. In the next section you will find step-by-step guides to eight character makeups. These will provide the basis for many of the roles you will want to play on stage. Used in conjunction with the personality variations on pages 48–59, they form a comprehensive character makeup reference.

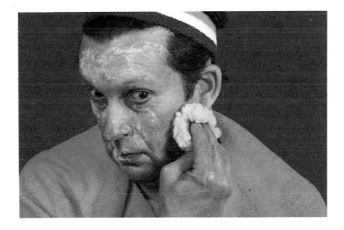

Ageing the Face

Ageing in both men and women is usually accompanied by a loss of fat from under the skin, a greying complexion, slackening muscles and deepening lines and furrows. This character makeup gives you that thin, grey, elderly face.

Add a little Blue lining colour to the base makeup for a grey skin tone. Strong shadows to the temples, eye-sockets, cheeks and neck help create a haggard face. Lines on the forehead and around the eyes, nose and mouth should be drawn in with a dark lining colour and they can be further emphasized by highlighting the areas in between, together with the brows, cheekbones, upper lip, nose and centre of the chin.

Always start by developing the shape and natural direction of the lines and folds that are already in your face. Pay special attention to the eyes, which must not look as though they are peering out through an elderly mask. Redden their rims with Crimson Lake and create the impression of sagging flesh by shading beneath them with lining colours.

With age, the teeth yellow and sometimes decay. Use black- or nicotine-coloured tooth enamel to give yourself a truly repellant smile.

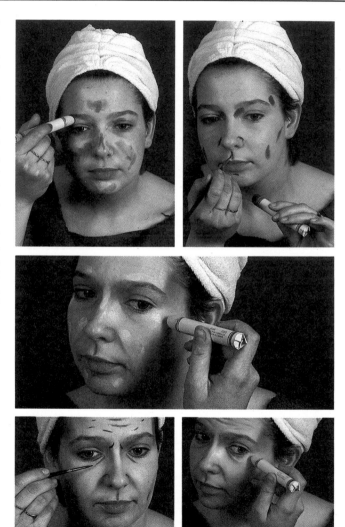

Top left Combine L No. 5, L No. 9 and K TZ Medium Blue to make a grey skin tone
Top right Apply a dark lining colour, L No. 7, to thin the face and to make existing shadows deeper
Centre Blend in the lining colour, and highlight with L No. 5
Right Use a mixture of L No. 7 and K TZ Crimson Lake for the fine lines on the forehead, nose and cheeks. Also use colour to create bags under the eyes
Far right Highlight your work with L No. 5

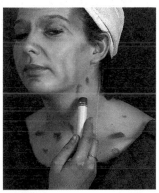

Top Now apply L No. 7 shadows to the neck, and highlight them with L No. 5. Apply an Aquacolour base of K 3W or K OA to the neck *Above* Powder and brush off. Strengthen lines and wrinkles with your brown wax pencil *Left* Touch in the lips with L Carmine 3 and use L No. 20 (White) to grey the eyebrows and eyelashes

A Younger Face

Smooth, taut skin and lips, prominent cheekbones, white teeth and thick glossy hair – a veteran actor in search of the fountain of youth need look no further than his makeup kit. For a few hours, at least, wrinkles, grey skin and sagging flesh caused by slack muscles can be made to disappear.

Use Kryolan TV White Aquacolour or a lighter colour than your base makeup to disguise furrows and wrinkles before applying the base colour. If the base is greasepaint, always use water-soluble makeup for this highlighting. Never put grease on grease, or water-base on water-base for this purpose because they will merge and the effect will be lost.

Compensate for any paleing of the skin with a healthy-looking base colour and apply colour to the cheeks to reintroduce the glow of youth. If your nose appears a little too old for the part, give it a younger look by shading along the sides. Use hair-colouring to eliminate greyness and, in extreme circumstances, tooth enamel to whiten the teeth.

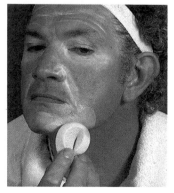

Far left Before beginning to make up, study your face and decide which base colour to use and which wrinkles and shadows you should eliminate
Above left Paint K TV White Aquacolour onto the darker areas and into the wrinkles of your face
Below left Use a light tone Aquacolour base – K 5L – to cover the beard shadow
Above right Apply a greasepaint base of L Nos 5 and 8, taking care not to disturb the Aquacolour groundwork
Right Use L No. 8 on both sides of the bridge of the nose to narrow it, and on the cheeks to give a youthful healthy glow

Left Use your black or brown pencil for the eyelines
Far left centre Paint in the lips with L No. 8. Generously powder and brush off the surplus
Far left below Reinforce the eyebrows with your black pencil
Centre left Now use a toothbrush to touch out any naturally grey hairs with Dark Brown Aquacolour, K No.102
Below left Alternatively, spray the hair with Dark Brown K aerosol spray, remembering to shield your eyes with a free hand or a card cutout. Comb the spray in well before it dries.

9 to 5, five days a week, but today *you* are the matinée idol!

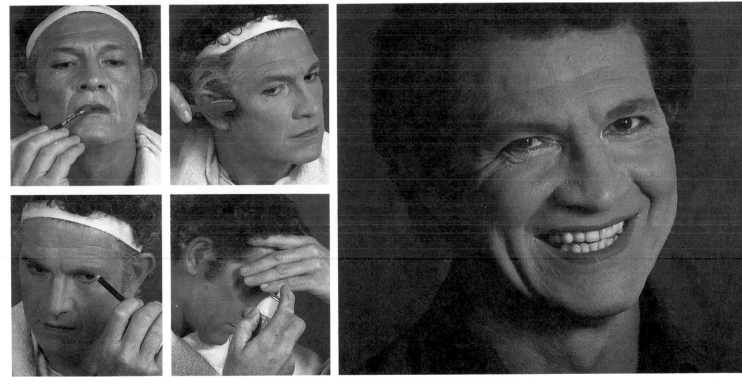

Thinning the Face

To make the face look thinner and narrower, use heavy shading to emphasize the bone structure rather than the flesh. All shaping should be vertical – use dark shading and lining colours to make the cheekbones more prominent and to thin the nose. For a more cadaverous appearance, shade the temple area and eye-sockets heavily too.

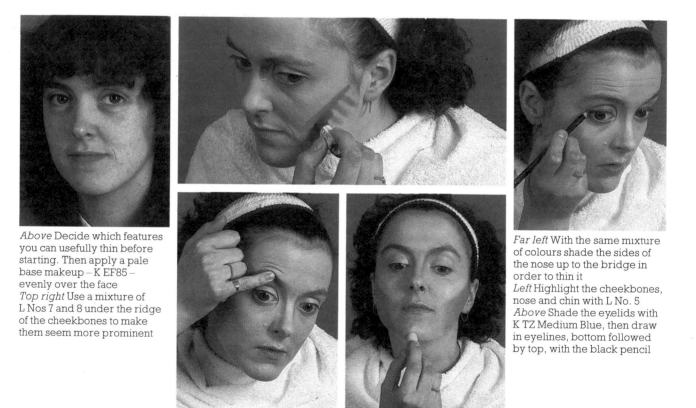

Above Decide which features you can usefully thin before starting. Then apply a pale base makeup – K EF85 – evenly over the face
Top right Use a mixture of L Nos 7 and 8 under the ridge of the cheekbones to make them seem more prominent

Far left With the same mixture of colours shade the sides of the nose up to the bridge in order to thin it
Left Highlight the cheekbones, nose and chin with L No. 5
Above Shade the eyelids with K TZ Medium Blue, then draw in eyelines, bottom followed by top, with the black pencil

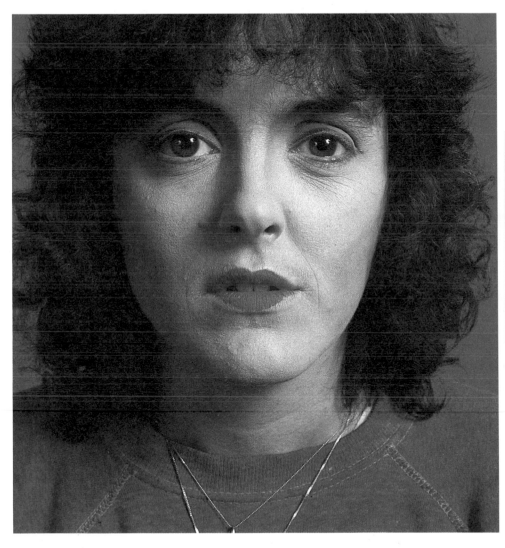

Above Shade the lips with K TZ Carmine and a No. 6 brush. Powder generously and brush off the surplus with the soft brush. Clean the eyelashes, apply a little mascara, and then touch in the eyebrows with the black, or brown, eyebrow pencil

Fattening the Face

To fatten your face, emphasize the flesh that already exists and, if necessary, create the illusion of extra flesh by shading and highlighting. Jowls and double chins can be suggested in this way too. In some cases you may want to create bags under the eyes with wax (see page 65), but usually it will be necessary simply to emphasize shadows with colour.

All shaping should be horizontal to make the face and neck appear fatter than they really are. Use horizontal lines on the cheeks and around the eyes, nose and mouth. Emphasize what flesh you have by shading around the cheeks and highlighting their centres.

Fat people often have ruddy complexions, so the choice of a deep-coloured base is appropriate, and use Crimson Lake or Rouge to redden the cheeks. Give yourself a florid, open-pored nose with Crimson Lake and a stipple sponge. The mouth should be full and red.

Two ways of fattening are demonstrated on these pages. The first shows how to make yourself fatter by emphasizing the flesh already on the face. The second shows how to grow old and fat with lines on the forehead and different shading and lining on the cheeks to give another interpretation.

Above right Cover the face with K F2 base and give form to the cheeks with L No. 9 applied horizontally from the nostrils to emphasize the width of the face
Right K TZ Crimson Lake lining is used to create jowls

Above left Highlight the nose, cheeks and jowls with L No. 5
Left Create the illusion of folds of fat on the neck with horizontal lines of Lake
Above Soften the edges of the neck lines and highlight them with L No. 5

Below To give the appearance of someone who is fatter *and* older, use Crimson Lake for wrinkles on the forehead and for the nose-mouth crease. Highlight with L No. 5
Bottom Use K TZ White to grey the eyebrows

Above Draw in eyelines with your black pencil and a full mouth with K TZ Carmine
Right Powder with translucent powder and brush off the excess. Reinforce the eyebrows with the brown pencil and restyle your hair

A Sad Face

Unhappy people tend to be pale and drawn. Their sorrow may be a result of some particular grief, it may be part of their nature, or it may be caused by illness and strain.

Choose a pale base and give the cheeks very little colour. Shape the corners of the eyes and mouth downwards, and emphasize the frown lines and the nose–mouth crease with Crimson Lake. Highlighting below the eyebrow will make the eyelid look heavier, as will shading of the eyebrow itself.

Top left Apply a pale base of K TV3 plus just a touch of L Carmine 2 to give a hint of colour to the cheeks
Left L No. 5 highlight below the eyebrow will make the eyelid seem heavier
Top With K TZ Crimson Lake, draw frown lines between the eyes, lines to emphasize the downward sweep of the nose–mouth crease, and others to extend and drop the corners of the mouth
Above Blend in the lining colour, and highlight your work with L No. 5

Below Draw in K TZ Black eyelines with a brush, dropping the corners of the eyes as you do so
Bottom Colour the lips with L Carmine 2, following the downward turn of the mouth. Dust the face heavily with translucent powder and brush away the surplus

Above Reinforce the eyebrows with your black pencil, dropping them to make you seem more depressed

A Happier Face

A happy face is a mobile one and often quite lined. By smiling, you rearrange the creases and shadows of the cheeks, you lift the corners of the mouth and eyes, and create "laugh-lines". Since a happy person has often escaped the strain of severe illness, skin and cheeks will be of a healthy colour.

All the shading on the face should work to lift the corners of the eyes, the eyebrows and the mouth. Use Eyebrow Plastic to alter the shape of the eyebrows if necessary. A light-coloured eyeshadow will counteract any heaviness of the eyelids, and Carmine will give the cheeks a rosy glow.

Right As one means of drawing attention to the eyes, the feature that best conveys an impression of mood, the eyebrows here have been slightly shortened with bar soap before the base of K F2 was laid down
Above Apply L Carmine 2 to colour the cheeks and blend it into the base. Its purpose is cosmetic rather than structural

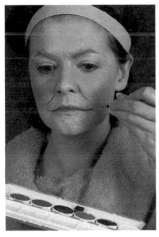

Left Shade the nose-mouth crease with K TZ Crimson Lake, shaping it outwards and upwards as it nears the mouth. Use the Lake to lift the corners of the mouth
Centre left Blend and then highlight the Crimson Lake work with L No. 5
Bottom left Apply L No. 336 (Green) to the eyelids and take it up and over that part of the eyebrows that has been abbreviated with the soap. This reduces any undue heaviness of the eyelids

Left Follow the uplifted corners of the mouth as you colour the lips with Carmine
Below left Draw the eyelines in K TZ Black, lower followed by upper as always, extending and lifting them at the outer corners
Above Clean your eyelashes of makeup and powder and touch in your eyebrows with a brown pencil

An Invalid

Unhealthiness, however slight, is usually apparent in the face. At the very least the sufferer will look sad and tired whilst prolonged illness leads to a loss of weight and the skin turns pale.

Mask out naturally healthy tones with a grey, pallid base colour. Deep shading and strong white highlights will emphasize the bone structure and

trim the face. White highlights and a thin application of white powder complete the picture.

Remember to make up the neck with a water-based colour equivalent to the pale greasepaint base. The unhealthy image will be ruined if your pale, grey face is sitting atop a glowing, healthy neck!

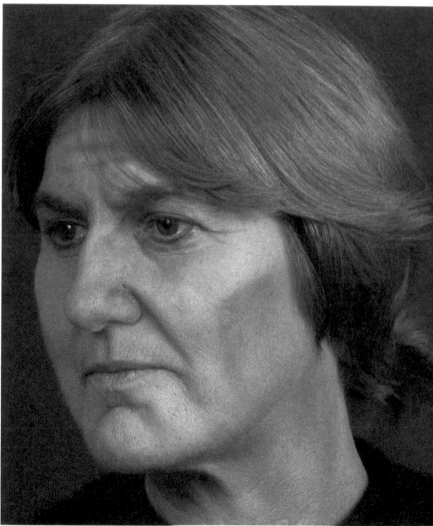

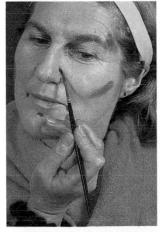

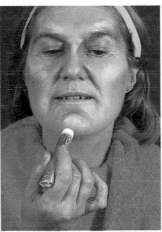

Left The component colours of this pallid complexion are L Nos 5 and 9 and a little K TZ Medium Blue. Mix them on the back of your hand if you are not sufficiently sure of the correct mixture to your face as a palette
Far left centre The shading, designed to make the face appear thin and drawn, is in L No. 7
Left centre With such a pale base (remember to colour your ears!) highlights of L No. 20 (pure White) will not look out of place

Left Use K TZ Black to intensify the deepest parts of the shadows
Top right Highlight under the eyes with L No. 20
Above Swamp the makeup with K TL1 (White) powder (one of the rare occasions when White should be used in preference to flesh-coloured powder), and brush off the surplus. Attend to your neck and hands and any other exposed parts of your body with K Ivory Aquacolour. For this particular characterization, the makeup of the neck can make an important contribution to the total effect

A Healthier Face

Good health is often only skin-deep on stage. With a little skill, even the sickliest actor can assume a ruddy complexion and a robust constitution.

Cover your skin with a healthy, glowing base colour and apply Carmine to the cheeks and chin. A touch of Medium Blue will make the eyelids seem less heavy and help to reduce the shadows in the eye-sockets. Make sure that your lips too are well coloured. And do not forget that a good head of thick, glossy hair can do wonders in deceiving a distant audience. A hairpiece or hair-colouring may be needed to complete the illusion of well-being.

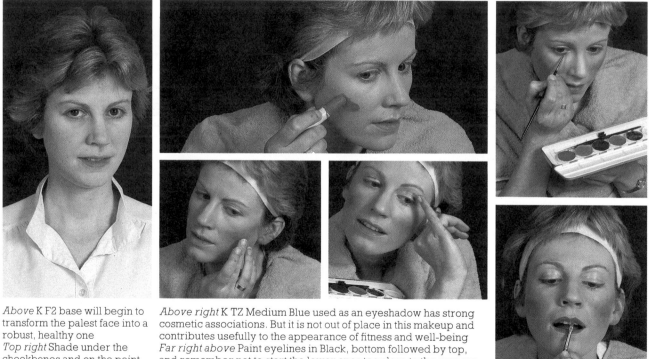

Above K F2 base will begin to transform the palest face into a robust, healthy one
Top right Shade under the cheekbones and on the point of the chin with L No. 9
Above centre right Strengthen the colour on the cheeks and chin with K TZ Carmine

Above right K TZ Medium Blue used as an eyeshadow has strong cosmetic associations. But it is not out of place in this makeup and contributes usefully to the appearance of fitness and well-being
Far right above Paint eyelines in Black, bottom followed by top, and remember not to start the lower ones too close to the corners of the eyes. It follows, since we almost always use eyelines simply to strengthen the visual containing effect of the lashes, that we should put them only where the lashes grow
Right Colour lips with Carmine and a No. 6 brush

Above Apply translucent powder generously, and brush off the excess. Clear the eyelashes of powder and makeup and apply mascara before finally reinforcing the eyebrows with the black pencil

Personality Traits

The previous chapter described how to create the characters you will play, in general terms of their age, stature, disposition and health. Once you have grasped these basic techniques, you will want to analyze your characters more deeply in order to portray some of their more subtle characteristics with your makeup.

What if you, as an averagely good-looking forty year old, are asked to play a handsome, pompous sixty-five year old? You know the techniques for ageing, and you must attend to your good features to make the most of them, but what can you do to make yourself look pompous? Or, as a delicate woman of forty yourself, you are given the role of a healthy, motherly type of that same age. You happen to be the correct age for the part, you have learned how to create an impression of well-being; how can you extend this to appear motherly as well?

This chapter gives a step-by-step guide to the creation of a number of commonly encountered personality traits. For each, there is a keyword followed by a number of related adjectives. The accompanying text and photographs show how to translate these words into images with the aid of your makeup. It is remarkable how few basic techniques are actually needed to create a range of such contrasting types.

Here is a summary of the personality traits dealt with in this chapter, followed by a brief description of how the makeup is done.

Keyword: Debauched Make the face look fatter and give the illusion of sagging jowls and skin. Beard shadow is applied round the outside edge of the face to emphasize its width. Cheek pouches, deep shadows round the eyes, a wide, red mouth and a stippled red nose and cheeks all contribute to a dissipated appearance. For a less debauched look, in other words to create an illusion of coarseness and vulgarity rather than dissipation, you should use less exaggerated colour on the nose and cheeks.

Keyword: Sophisticated Sophisticated people tend often to be careful about their appearance, paying close attention to details of makeup, hair and clothing. In this example the cheekbones have been heightened and the nose thinned and shortened with Leichner No. 9. For a male subject, the shaping and shading would be the same, but the use of Leichner No. 7 would be appropriate.

Keyword: Eccentric Give the face a wild surprised expression with discordant shading, highlighting and lining. A cleft chin, rosebud mouth and unkempt hair are used here to create an appearance of eccentricity.

Keyword: Conventional Make the character as mundane as possible by doing nothing to enhance any of the features. Use a pale base and do not shade the cheekbones. Make sure that the eyes are dulled by choosing a neutral coloured eyeshadow and by applying only a bottom eyeline.

By carrying this makeup one stage further, a completely different image – that of a "Simple Simon" or the village idiot – can be achieved. Slightly raise foreshortened eyebrows and use the device of "crossing the eyes" – drawing a vertical line down the eyelids and below the eyes – to create a comic appearance of gentle idiocy.

Keyword: Mean For a fierce, hard-faced man, shade the face heavily, as for ageing, in order to emphasize the shape of the skull, but not to draw attention to wrinkles or lines. Create sagging flesh under the eyes and around the nose and mouth. Narrow the lips and, for the complete villain, make sure that the eyebrows are heavy and arched.

For a sly, cunning expression, you will need to drop the corners of the eyes more than those illustrated on page 52, and increase the strength of the highlight on the eyelids to make the eyes look less pronounced and more sinister. Make the mouth narrower and use no colour on the lips.

Keyword: Naïve An appearance of open-faced innocence depends greatly upon trusting eyes. The eyebrows should not be heavy – use Eyebrow Plastic or bar soap if necessary. Shade and highlight only the eyes; no other shaping should be done, but apply cheek colouring generously over the whole cheek area. The photograph here illustrates a character who would normally use makeup. A child or man should substitute blue shadow for brown around the eyes and use less cheek and eye colour.

Keyword: Austere Characteristics such as austerity and cynicism become more apparent with increasing age. In creating the cold, hard business-man on page 54, it was necessary to age the subject with a heavier beard shadow, an emphasized nose–mouth crease, and heavier lining. An older actor might need only to accentuate his features.

Keyword: Spinsterish For a sharp-featured and slightly shrewish spinster, create a thin, pinched face. Dropped corners to the eyes and mouth, flared nostrils, strengthened eyebrows and pale lips will suggest an older, frustrated woman.

Keyword: Motherly Generous and gentle, happy and healthy – how many mothers can truly claim to be "motherly"? A good cheek colour, soft grey eyeshadow, full, smiling lips and laugh-lines will all help to create this elusive ideal.

Keyword: Depressed Carry one step further the unhappy character makeup from the previous chapter, dropping the corners of the eyes and mouth more, and shading the nose–mouth crease more heavily. For the purposes of a stage performance, the physical evidence of depression comes with a pale skin, so choose a suitable light-coloured base. Apply a dark colour to the eyelids to sink the eyes back into their sockets and shade under the eyes to create eyebags. A thinned lower lip will help to give the face a pinched appearance.

Keyword: Pompous Make the face florid and disdainful by reddening the cheeks, curling up the corners of the lips, and emphasizing the nose–mouth crease. A cleft chin, as illustrated in this example, seems to suggest haughtiness and the pomposity of the character is somehow endorsed by giving the hair a centre parting.

Keyword: Tarty Depending upon the degree of tartiness of your character, this makeup can be quite coarse and overstated. Colour the cheeks with Carmine, and create the illusion of eyebags. A harder mouth, nose and eyebrows than were used in this makeup will suggest a tougher person.

Debauched

dissipated
coarse, vulgar, corrupt
lascivious

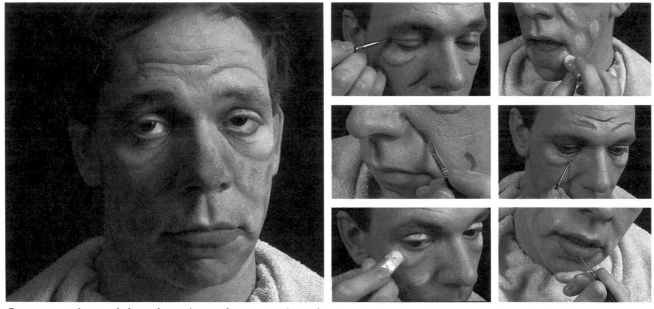

On stage, at least, debauchery is as often a comic trait as a villainous one. Shakespeare's Falstaff is as debauched, and as beloved, as any character in theatrical history. But the stage (especially in Victorian times) has also given us vile seducers and depraved alcoholics. This mixed-up morality does not greatly affect the makeup: sagging jowls, red eyes and a coarse complexion remain the same.

From top to bottom The base is L Nos 5 and 8 with a little K TZ Medium Blue. Lines are drawn well above the lashlines on the top lids. Create eyebags with L No. 7. Use this tone for the nose-mouth creases which be spread outwards and upwards. Highlight with L No. 5

From top to bottom Complete the highlighting. Line with K TZ Crimson Lake. Shade the chin and extend the corners of the mouth with L No. 7. Paint the lips and stipple nose and cheeks with Crimson Lake. Powder on, brush off, then eyelashes and eyebrows

Sophisticated

**experienced, smooth, smart, well-groomed
organized, clever, ambitious, brisk, elegant
classy, stylish, self-assured, single-minded
self-sufficient, well-bred, cool
worldly, confident**

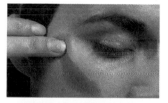

Top right Onto a base of K 12, apply L No. 9, L No. 7 for men, to the sides of the bridge of the nose and high on the cheeks to lift the cheekbones. Now smooth a little L No. 7 on the eyelids. *Centre right* Draw in the eyelines heavily with the black pencil, extending and lifting them slightly at the outer corners of the eyes

This makeup spans a wide spectrum of related traits, from the comic cynicism of Algernon Moncrieff and John Worthing in *The Importance of Being Earnest* to the brisk efficiency of Maggie in Harold Brighouse's *Hobson's Choice* or the self-sufficiency of Eliza Doolittle in G. B. Shaw's *Pygmalion*. Attention to the details of makeup and costume will contribute to an impression of worldliness and style.

Above Highlight immediately below the eyebrows and on the bridge of the nose with K TZ White. Colour the lips with Carmine 2, powder and brush away the surplus. Clean the eyelashes, use mascara and touch in the eyebrows. You Star!

Eccentric

**vague, senile, excitable, foolish
silly, difficult, forgetful, twittish, whimsical
temperamental, dotty, empty-headed
affected, bumbling**

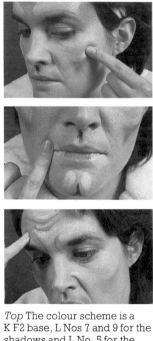

Below left Use a mixture of K TZ Crimson Lake and L No. 7 to shape the forehead with strongly curving lines that reflect heavy brows and a prominent cranium. Underline the eyes and reinforce the shape of the nostrils and the nose-mouth crease. Highlight this work with L No. 5
Below Dab a little Carmine 2 onto the cheeks, no need for any great precision here; but the mouth, also in Carmine 2, should be drawn in with care. Swamp with translucent powder, brush off the surplus, clean your eyelashes of powder and touch in your eyebrows with a black pencil. You are dealing here with characteristics that provide wonderful opportunities for some creative work on the hair, perhaps with a wig if your own is too restrained for the part

Top The colour scheme is a K F2 base, L Nos 7 and 9 for the shadows and L No. 5 for the highlights.
Centre Emphasize the vertical divide below the nose, give form to a cleft chin and reduce the width of the mouth with L No. 5

Eccentricity is a catch-all quality, ranging from mere forgetfulness to lunacy. This makeup can express the twittishness of Canon Throbbing in Alan Bennett's *Habeas Corpus*, or the senility of Maud in Peter Nichol's *Born in the Gardens*. It can also be used to create very theatrical eccentrics like Agatha Christie's Miss Marple, and the Noël Coward spiritualists, Madame Arcati and Miss Erikson.

Conventional

ordinary, plain, insignificant
conservative, quiet, common-sensical, neat
boring, sober, solid, mousey, uneducated
simple

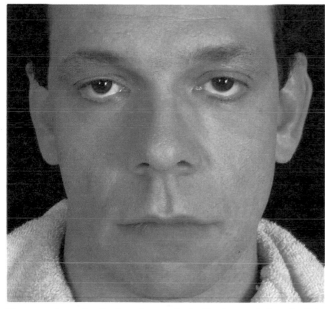

Some plays include characters that are intended to appear physically unremarkable. From the mousey teenager Mary Mooney in Mary O'Malley's *Once a Catholic* to the conventional Son in John Mortimer's *A Voyage Round My Father*, the makeup should be minimal, with no shaping of the features at all.

The "Simple Simon" look is appropriate, for example, for the Scarecrow in *The Wizard of Oz*.

Top Apply a pale base of K 7W, carrying the colour over the eyebrows to reduce their dominance – it is not always necessary to use Eyebrow Plastic or bar soap as a preliminary step to achieve this effect. L No. 7 is used as eyeshadow above the eyes and for eyelines below them
Above L No. 8 on the lips provides the right strength of tone without being too colourful. Fix the makeup thoroughly with a heavy dusting of translucent powder, brush away the excess, clean the eyelashes and reinforce the eyebrows

Above Accentuate and arch the eyebrows, and draw a vertical line down the centre of each of the upper lids, extending these lines below the eyes. This is a simple device and one which has always proves very effective on stage.

Mean

**nasty, spiteful, bitter, misanthropic
embittered, subtle, shifty
cunning, sinister, greedy, bullying
evil, frightening**

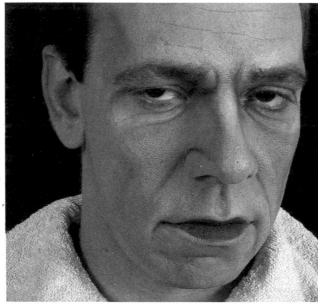

Villainy comes in many forms. The principles of this make up will provide a suitable starting-point for characters as diverse as the frightening and cruel Bill Sykes in *Oliver*; the murderous Sweeney Todd; the sinister, off-beat figures of Roat in Frederick Knott's *Wait Until Dark* and Jack Manningham in Patrick Hamilton's Victorian drama *Gaslight*; and the greedy bully Gaston Lemare in *My Three Angels*.

From top to bottom The base is a mixture of L Nos 5 and 8 made less colourful with the addition of a little K TZ Medium Blue. Introduce a heavy beard tone of Medium Blue and model the features strongly with shadows of L No. 7 and highlights of L No. 5.

Accentuate the deepest areas of shadow, and strengthen the lines in the face with K TZ Crimson Lake. The object is to create the impression of heavy, sagging flab. Blend the colour in and highlight the work with L No. 5.

Keep well within the natural fullness of the lips to create a tight, mean-looking mouth with K TZ Crimson Lake. Fix the makeup with a generous dusting of translucent powder and brush away the surplus

Clear your eyelashes of powder and add weight and thickness to your eyebrows with the black pencil. Remember to sponge Aquacolour onto your ears, neck and hands, and onto any other parts of your body which would otherwise be revealed in all of their natural pallor!

Naïve

innocent, frank, honest, direct
quiet, reserved, weak, open-faced, uncertain
fresh-faced, empty-headed, shy, childlike
day-dreamer, moonfaced

Below Use Eyebrow Plastic or dampened bar soap to reduce the weight of thick eyebrows before applying a base of K 3W. Complete the reduction of the eyebrows with a dense application of L No. 5
Top right Shade the eyelids with K TZ Medium Blue, taking the colour up to the new line of the eyebrows. Highlight with L No. 20 (White)
Centre right Draw in eyelines heavily with the Medium Blue, extending and lifting them at the corners

Naïvite is childlike but not therefore childish. The face that is untouched by cynicism or guilt, the eyes that are frank and inquiring – this makeup is used to express the innocence to be found in adults as well as in the young. Clifford Bradshaw, the unsophisiticated young Englishman in the musical *Cabaret*, is as much a child in his corrupt environment as is young Oliver Twist in Victorian London.

Above Shade the cheeks with L No. 9, spreading the colour well down towards the line of the jaw. Use Carmine 2 for the lips, powder to fix the makeup and then brush away the excess. Clean your eyelashes and stengthen eyebrows with your black or brown pencil

Austere

**aggressive, hard, determined, cold, severe,
ruthless, strong, formidable, assertive, authoritative
domineering, serious, purposeful, stubborn
dominating, powerful, impressive**

Top Apply a base of L Nos 5 and 8 cooled with a touch of K TZ Medium Blue. Work more Medium Blue into the base to establish a beard shadow. Shadows on the sides of the temples and the bridge of the nose, as well as ageing lines on the forehead and below the eyes are all K TZ Coffee Brown. Nothing has been done to emphasize the structure of the cheekbones
Below K TZ Coffee Brown is also used to accent the nose-mouth creases and to turn down the corners of a humourless mouth. Highlight all your shadow work with L No. 5
Far right Powder heavily, with the translucent kind, and brush away the surplus. You may develop the character a little more with a crêpe hair, or ready-made moustache (see pages 60–63), and by using some K TZ White to grey the sideburns, the eyebrows, and the moustache

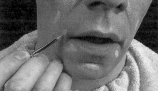

With these makeup techniques you can portray characters as diverse as the hard businessman portrayed above, the pleasant, strong-minded Monica Reed in Noël Coward's *Present Laughter*, and the formidable Lady Bracknell in Oscar Wilde's *The Importance of Being Earnest*. For these last two, however, you would not turn down the corners of the mouth.

Spinsterish

**sex-starved, shrewish
fussy, repressed, prudish
interfering**

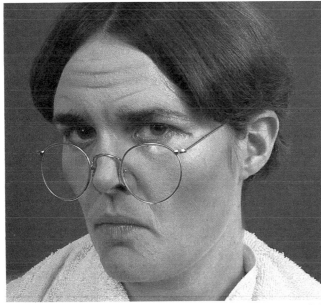

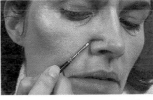

There are a number of variations on this spinsterish makeup. The typical, fussy spinster is wonderfully caricatured in Constance Wickstead from Alan Bennett's *Habeas Corpus*, but these techniques will also prove useful for the frustrated and cruel Nurse Ratched in Dale Wesserman's *One Flew Over the Cuckoo's Nest*. Do not forget that men, although never spinsters, can be just as fussy as women.

Top Mix a base of K 3W with a little K TV White. Shade into this with L No. 7 on the temples, under the cheekbones and around the eyes. Use the same colour for lining the forehead, accentuating the nostrils, and extending the mouth
Above Highlight with L No. 5
Top right Intensify the blended shadows, underline the eyes to add some puffiness, softly outline the upper lip and drop the corners of the mouth, all with K TZ Crimson Lake
Centre right Drop the outer corners of the eyes with a touch of Crimson Lake

Above Use the Lake to give more shape to the chin. Now, with a black pencil, flare the nostrils and draw in a vertical line below the nose. Finally, drench your work with powder, brush off and attend to your eyelashes and eyebrows

Motherly

**pleasant, kindly, jolly, placid, contented
loving, sympathetic, cheerful, easy-going
affectionate, well-meaning, gentle, generous,
protective, tolerant, patient, amiable**

Top Over a base of K F2, colour the cheeks with L No. 9 mixed with Carmine 2
Centre Lighten K TZ Black with White to make a soft grey eyeshadow. Use K TZ Medium Blue for the eyelines
Above Crimson Lake should be used as a lining colour

Motherliness, in its purest sense, combines radiant good health with an abundance of mature, unselfish love that extends far beyond a woman's immediate family. But you do not need to be a mother to possess many motherly qualities. The kindly witch Glinda from *The Wizard of Oz*, even men, such as jolly old Mr Fezziwig from *A Christmas Carol*, can benefit from the principles of this makeup.

Top See how the Crimson Lake is used to abbreviate the nose-mouth crease and outline the lips
Centre Highlight your work with L No. 5
Above Make the lips full with Carmine 2. Powder, brush off, eyelashes and eyebrows

Depressed

miserable, gloomy, haggard, tense
discouraged, strained, lonely, touchy, worried
harassed, self-torturing
manically depressed

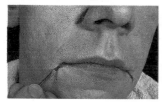

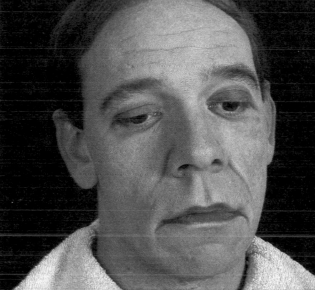

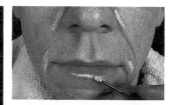

Top Depression is a mood well conveyed on the stage by a pallid complexion, so apply that very light-coloured base, K 7W. A strongly contrasting beard shadow is achieved with K TZ Medium Blue. Eyeshadow, bottom and then top eyelines, dropped at the corners, and heavy bags under the eyes are all stated with L No. 7. You should apply this colour with the aid of either of your brushes
Above Make the corners of the mouth appear to droop and accentuate the nose-mouth creases all with L No. 7

Jeanette Fisher in Neil Simon's *The Last of the Red Hot Lovers* and Wilfred Shadbolt in *The Yeomen of the Guard* are typical of the depressed character portrayed here. Heavier lining will give the worried expression of Hedley in Peter Nichol's *Born in the Gardens*, while heavier shading will produce the manic depression of Mr Purdue in Alan Bennett's *Habeas Corpus*.

Top Highlight the shadow work with L No. 5, using this colour to reduce the fullness of the bottom lip and to make the mouth appear to be thinner. Use Carmine 3, the darkest of all the Carmines, for the lips
Above Having sealed the makeup with a liberal dusting of translucent powder, brush off the excess and, when reinforcing the eyebrows with the black pencil, extend and drop them to echo the unhappy mood of the eyes. Clear your eyelashes of any makeup or powder which may have stuck to them

Pompous

**proud, ponderous, arrogant, conceited
sel-important, staid, complacent, opinionated
snobbish, loud, brash
portentous**

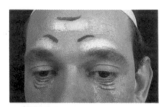

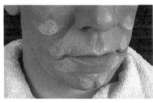

Left The base colour is a mixture of L Nos 5 and 8, the beard shadow reinstated with K TZ Medium Blue and, to impart a florid glow, the cheeks are daubed with L No. 8 brightened up with K TZ Crimson Lake. The shadows are L No. 7, also reddened by the addition of Crimson Lake. The work is highlighted with L No. 5
Centre left Begin to convey the impression of a wide, fleshy mouth by extending and curling up the corners. A cleft chin is not in itself a mark of pomposity but the sense of puffiness it adds to the face as a whole, is useful. Powder and brush off
Below left For a colour so strong, Crimson Lake is surprisingly versatile and very useful. Here, as a lip colour, it is used to complete a heavy, full mouth *after* powdering, to retain all the richness of the colour. Finally, attend to the eyelashes and eyebrows, as ever

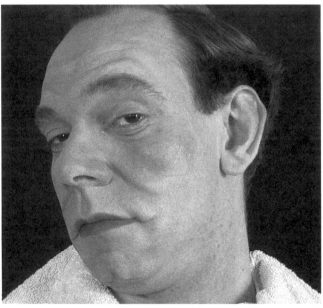

Pomposity – that familiar compound of conceit and stupidity – is well represented on stage. It is the predominant characteristic of Mr Bumble in *Oliver* and Alderman Joseph Helliwell in J. B. Priestley's *When We Are Married*. It is also present in the arrogance of Garry Essendine in Noël Coward's *Present Laughter* and the ponderous self-importance of Sven in Alan Ayckbourn's *Joking Apart*.

Tarty

**cheap, without taste, bitchy
outrageous, flirtatious, common
hard, flamboyant
decadent**

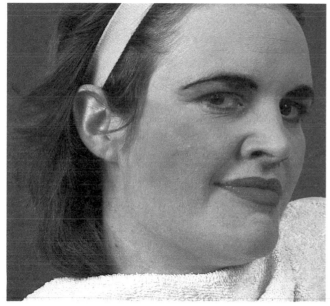

Below Over a base of K F2, apply L No. 9 mixed with Carmine 2 to brightly colour the cheeks. Shade under the eyes and around the nostrils with K TZ Crimson Lake
Bottom Outline the bottom lip generously with Crimson Lake to make it fuller
Top right Blend the shadow colour evenly into the base, and highlight the work with L No. 5
Centre right Mix a thunderous eyeshadow of K TZ Black and Crimson Lake and carry it up across the eyelids

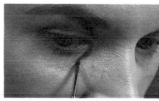

This makeup can be used to good effect for characters like Rita in *Billy Liar* or Mary McGinty in *Once a Catholic*. The heaviness of the lip and eye makeup is also appropriate for the panache of showgirl Roxie Hart in *Chicago*, or the absence of colour sense in Beverley from Mike Leigh's *Abigail's Party*, but in these cases the hardness in the shaping of the eyebrows and nose should be reduced.

Above Using your No. 6 brush, paint in full, luscious lips with K TZ Carmine. Drench your tarty face in translucent powder, brush away the surplus, clean and mascara your eyelashes, and strengthen your eyebrows with the aid of the black pencil

The Use of Special Materials

Some stage roles call for a more radical alteration to the appearance of an actor than can be achieved in greasepaint alone. To this end, it is possible to use putty and wax to remodel your features (see pages 64–65), crêpe hair or a hairpiece to embellish a clean-shaven actor, a wig or a bald cap for a special effect.

Wig blocks, traditionally sculpted in wood, are used to support wigs and hairpieces. There are now three types of block in use, wooden, malleable and polystyrene – and they serve three distinct purposes. The wooden blocks are used only in the making of wigs. The malleable blocks, made of cork and covered with a heavy linen, are used when dressing or styling a wig, when the ability to stick pins into the cork base to secure a wig or rollers is an obvious advantage. The third type of block, made from expanded polystyrene, is used simply for supporting a wig whenever it is not in use. These blocks should never be allowed to come into contact with direct heat.

A good wig which has been especially made for you, should fit your head snugly, but of course it can only do so if you have provided the wig-maker with these essential measurements:

i) The circumference of the head. This maximum dimension is measured from the centre of the forehead, ½ inch below the hairline (balding men may need to dig deep into their memories), over the top of the ears, around the back of the head and back to the centre of the forehead.

ii) The longitudinal dimension. From the same frontal centrepoint, over the top of the head and down to the nape of the neck.

iii) The transverse dimension. Across the top of the head, from ear to ear.

Wigs and Hairpieces

Wigs

You can hire and buy three kinds of wigs: those with a lace front, those without a front, and those with a material front.

Lace-front and front-less wigs The term "lace-front" comes from the period when wigs had fronts made from handwoven lace of human hair. The material which is used today is a machine-made gauze or net. Lace-front and frontless wigs are put on the head after the face and neck have been made up. If the wig needs any adhesive to hold it in place, only ever use spirit gum – rubber adhesive cannot be successfully removed and you are likely to damage the wig in the process of trying. To anchor the wig, you are unlikely to need more than a small dab of gum on the forehead and one in front of each ear. If you use too much gum, you risk it being seen.

Material-fronted wigs Sometimes the setting or context of a play demands the use of a wig with a linen or silk front. These wigs are made on a base which is thicker than that used for the other two types, and so will certainly need to be secured with spirit gum. Unlike its kin, the material-fronted wig must always be fixed in position before the makeup is begun, so that the material front may be included as part of the head to be disguised with makeup.

Hairpieces

There are a number of different hairpieces (see right), but the most frequently used are beards, moustaches, switches, curls and falls.

Lace beards and moustaches Always attach these hairpieces with a thin film of spirit gum after the face has been made up. When they are not being used, keep them pinned to a block or safely in a box.

Switches, curls and falls These additions are fixed with hairpins or tied on with a few strands of your own hair. Just like all other hairpieces, they should be packed away carefully when not in use.

Dressing and styling
The wig or hairpiece is first pinned to a malleable block. Comb water or hairdresser's gel into the hair before using rollers or tape to hold it in position. You may safely use a hair-drier, curling tongs or heated rollers on human-hair wigs or hairpieces, but you certainly may not do so on those made of acrylic plastics, which will quickly melt with the heat. You may *never* wash, cut or restyle hired hairpieces or wigs. If the wig is yours, follow the manufacturer's cleaning instructions.

Putting on and taking off
Wigs Grasp the wig firmly at the back edge – not by the hair alone – and pull it over the head from the front until the hairline is in place. Use your tail-comb to settle the hairs that will be displaced. Remove the wig, again by holding its back edge with both hands, and pull it forward over and off the head.

Beards and moustaches Apply a film of spirit gum to the area of the face upon which the beard or moustache will rest. Allow the gum to become slightly tacky, then press the gauze firmly onto it. When the piece is in position, comb the hairs with the tail-comb, being careful not to snag the gauze. To remove the hairpiece, dab spirit gum solvent onto the gummed surfaces, wait for a few minutes and then gently pull it off the face. Alternatively, you may carefully peel off the hairpiece and then attend to the gum remaining on your face with solvent.

Loose Hairwork

Crêpe hair, made of wool, comes in various shades and in crimped strands of up to eight inches long that are braided with string into a longer plait. To make a beard, you will need at least two shades of hair of the colour you are using, the lighter shade to be used over the darker layer. Cut and remove the string holding the plait before attempting to separate the hair from it. Fan the end of the plait and pull out the hair you need, use the material at full length, and trim it on the face.

Top row, from left to right Build the basis of the beard with three sections of hair gummed to the underside of the jaw. Brush a film of spirit gum onto the upper surfaces of the jawline. Firm flats of crêpe hair in position, again in three broad sections. Now apply a layer of less dense grey hair over the dark foundation

Bottom row, from left to right Construct the moustache, one side at a time, overlaying brown base hair with grey. Beginning with the moustache, trim away surplus hair. When the beard has been trimmed to its final shape, K TV White Aquacolour streaks in the hair and a pair of spectacles complete the transformation

Wax An open wound

Kryolan Special Wax and Naturo Plasto are much softer materials than the makeup artist's putty. Because they are easier to work with, they may be used on fleshy as well as bony parts of the face.

These waxes are self-adhesive but must always be pressed firmly onto clean skin. Like putty, they can be applied, then cut and coloured for a painless 'wound'. Simulate bruising by stippling with Medium

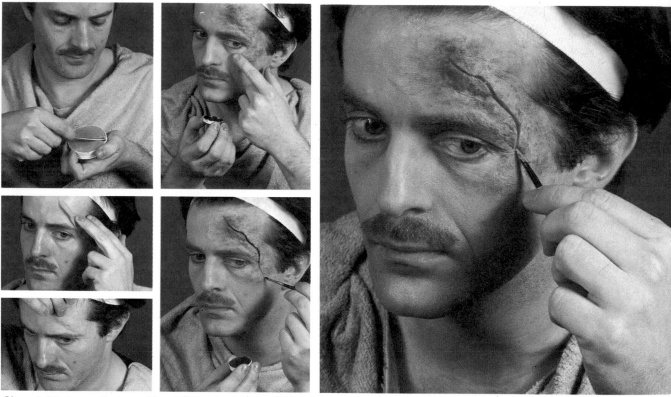

Above left Roll a small piece of Special Wax into a thin strip *Centre left* Press the strip in place onto clean skin *Below left* Smooth the edges of the wax and brush with Sealor to prevent any change in the colour of the base which may now be applied

Above left "Bruising" is achieved with K TZ Medium Blue, Crimson Lake and Black. *Above* Form the "cut" with a blunt, pointed object *Below left* Use Crimson Lake and a little removing cream to simulate flowing blood, or use a proprietary blood

A simple nose job

Blue, Crimson Lake and Black from the Kryolan TZ palette. To change the shape of a nose, apply a thin strip vertically for a lean, emaciated look, and horizontally for a broader shape.

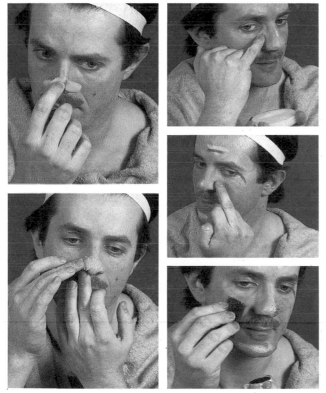

Above left Flatten the centre of a thin strip of wax and press it in place *Below left* Mould the wax to the nose *Above right* Soften the edges with the help of removing cream *Centre right* After Sealor, apply the base colour *Below right* Stipple with Lake

Bags of wax

When any work with wax is completed, brush it with Sealor to ensure that the makeup, when applied, will lose none of its colour.

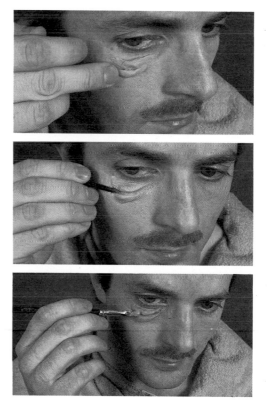

Above Press two thin strips of wax firmly in place onto clear skin *Centre* Mould and shape the wax with the end of a brush *Below* Brush the work with Sealor and define the eyebags with Crimson Lake

Bald Caps

Latex or plastic caps that cover the head like bathing-caps can be used for many purposes – from the foundation of a wig or hairpiece to special effects such as the ethereal being demonstrated here. Bald caps mould to the shape of the head. Excess material should be trimmed off with the cap in position. Apply spirit gum to the forehead and sides of the face to hold the cap in place but always try on the cap to see where it comes in contact with the face before applying the spirit gum to those areas. Conceal the thickish edge of an inexpensive cap with a smear of Eyebrow Plastic.

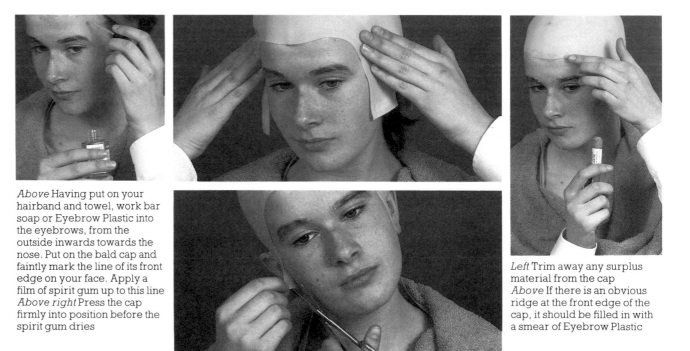

Above Having put on your hairband and towel, work bar soap or Eyebrow Plastic into the eyebrows, from the outside inwards towards the nose. Put on the bald cap and faintly mark the line of its front edge on your face. Apply a film of spirit gum up to this line
Above right Press the cap firmly into position before the spirit gum dries

Left Trim away any surplus material from the cap
Above If there is an obvious ridge at the front edge of the cap, it should be filled in with a smear of Eyebrow Plastic

Below left Sponge K Aquacolour TV White onto the cap.
(Greasepaint would be absorbed by the latex and fail to cover.)
Bottom left Cover the face with the TV White. Do not forget the
ears. Swamp the makeup with White powder and brush off any
surplus before proceeding to the final stages
Below right K No. 336 (Green) brushed on the eyelids provides
a dramatic contrast
Bottom right Use K TZ Black for the eyelines and paint in full lips
with L Carmine 3

Draw in the eyebrows and make up the neck with
Aquacolour to complete the ethereal effect

Traditional and Fantasy Makeup

You should now be equipped with the knowledge of how to make up for most of the character parts you are likely to play. It is probable however that, having mastered these basic techniques, you will want to apply them more imaginatively to some traditional and some fantasy creatures of your own devising.

Racial makeup

If the role you are to play on stage is racially other than your own, you must decide which are the physical characteristics which typify that race – the colour of skin, the shape of the skull, the hair, the shape and colour of the eyes, the nose and the mouth; consider them all. If you need to portray a Nordic character, for example, the stage stereotype is of one who is tall and slim, with a pale skin, a long narrow face and blond hair. A North American Indian has a deeply tanned skin, prominent cheekbones and straight, jet-black hair. The most telling facial characteristics of the white Anglo-Saxon are the pale skin colour, the brown hair and the smallish features.

On pages 72–73 and 76–77 we deal with the Latin and Oriental. In each case, a white Anglo-Saxon actress was chosen so as to show how dramatically and convincingly quite fundamental changes of racial type can be made with greasepaint.

Traditional Makeup

It is of course essential that the characters you create for the stage fit the audience's conception of them; that is the principal purpose behind these very largely symbolic makeups. Use all the references you can find.

On pages 74–75 and 78–80 we deal with two traditional types, Mephistopheles and the Pantomime Dame. In the former, emphasis has been put on shading and highlighting the centre of the face; for the latter, the sex of the actor has been allowed to shine through the makeup quite deliberately. Remember, this character is always the Dame who never is!

Animal Makeup

Animal makeup is mostly a matter of finding a costume that will fit you as well as it fits the part you are to play. Most costumes are all-enveloping but we are concerned in this book with those that, at least in part, leave the face exposed. Think of a rabbit and you will probably see a pair of enormous floppy ears and two massive front teeth. If it is Dick Whittington's companion that you are playing, then it may be the eyes and the whiskers that come to mind. Work boldly, you are creating images in which there is no place for fine detail.

Fantasy Makeup

Now you can really give vent to your imagination and draw upon the examples set by clowns, mime and street-theatre artists.

A green base and chiselled features transform the young actress on page 70 into the mischevious pixie on page 71; and just look at the disembodied apparition on pages 66–67. You can use Kryolan's glitter makeups to advantage (see page 71). You may have the opportunity to experiment with Kryolan's phosphorescent Luminous Makeup which glows in the dark for between three and five minutes, or their fluorescent Luminous Makeup, of which the stunning effect is seen only under strong ultra-violet light.

A Puckish Pixie

Below Always make sure that your hair is kept well clear of your face with a hairband or net

Right Apply Eyebrow Plastic or bar soap to flatten the eyebrows, working in short strokes inwards towards the centre. Work with the direction of the hairs, starting at the outer ends of the brows, in short strokes, each successive stroke slightly overlapping the previous one

Centre right Mix K 336 (Green) with K TZ White for the kind of complexion every self-respecting pixie craves. Concentrate the colours towards the centre of the face and blend them outwards. If you are not confident of achieving the tone of colour you are aiming for, mix the ingredients on the back of your hand

Below centre and below right Shape the brow in a continuous sweep from the bridge of the nose and accentuate the cheekbones with L No. 7

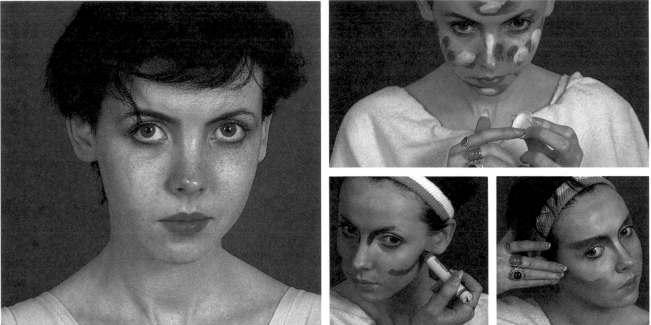

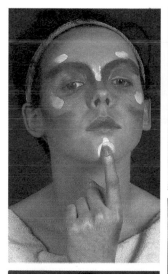

Far left Highlight the face with K TZ White

Below left Draw in the eyelines with K TZ Black, taking the top one above the lashline, up onto the centre of the lid. Extend both eyelines well beyond the corners of the eyes, and allow them to follow the shading over the brow. Draw in another line of Black, from the bridge of the nose along the top edge of the brown tone

Left Fill between the eyelines with K TZ White and paint the lips with L No. 7, extending and slightly lifting the corners of the mouth. Swamp with translucent powder and brush off the surplus

Below Make up the neck with a thin application of K Aquacolour No. 512, putting form and structure into it with K Aquacolour No. 102. Highlight the cheeks and shoulders with a light sprinkling of K Green and Gold Glitter

The Inscrutable Countenance

Top The shape of the features will need modification for this makeup to be convincing
Above Mask out the eyebrows totally with Eyebrow Plastic or bar soap
Top right Apply a base of K Ivory paintstick or L No. 5, taking the colour over the eyebrows
Centre right Cover the lips with the base colour

Left Shade horizontally below the cheekbones with L No. 8 to emphasize the roundness we associate with the Oriental face. Blend the Golden Tan upwards slightly, so that it gives colour as well as form to the cheeks
Top left Highlight your work with L No. 5 above the cheekbones, down the ridge of the nose and across the temples
Above left Use your black pencil to draw in almond-shaped eyes. This is a very significant feature of the makeup
Top right The eyelids are heavily highlighted with the Ivory paintstick so as to reduce the prominence of the brows above them
Above right Lips, drawn in with Carmine 2, can be very small and delicately shaped

Top Smother the makeup heavily with translucent powder and gently brush off the surplus

Above Draw in shortened eyebrows which should be positioned higher on the brow than those they replace. With a little more thought and some black hair spray, the model's soft brown hair can be styled for a worthy deception

Top Apply K TV White evenly over the face and neck
Centre Use K TZ Medium Blue to accent the beard shadow. It is essential to do a complete makeup even though a crêpe beard and moustache are to be added finally
Right Add broad strokes of tone in K TZ Crimson Lake and strengthen this modelling with touches of K TZ Black applied carefully with your No. 2 brush

Mephistopheles

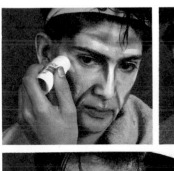

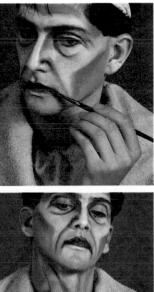

Top left Blend the shadow colours into the base and highlight with TV White *Top right* Areas of the most intense shadow may now be re-emphasized in Black and smoothed in *Above* Now define the shape of the eyes with your black pencil

Top Extend and drop the corners of the mouth with Crimson Lake *Centre* Use TV White and Crimson Lake to give form to the neck *Right* Apply translucent powder liberally to fix the greasepaint and then brush away the surplus

Top After powdering, use the black pencil to flare the nostrils and dramatize the eyebrows
Above Begin to construct the beard; refer to pages 62–63 for the details. You can see from this series of step-by-step photographs, and from others in the book, how the vision of the developing makeup seems to carry the actor into the role he is preparing to play

The Mediterranean Type

To achieve convincingly the appearance of a character of different nationality from yourself, you must look for the differences in features and skin colour. To create the Latin look, use the olive-coloured base K F7 for the new skin tone, shadows and highlight to lengthen the nose, and eyebrow pencil to strengthen the eyebrows.

 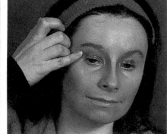

Above This is a makeup which needs an Olive base, conveniently available in the form of K F7 for those who prefer not to tackle the job of mixing it for themselves
Right above Shade under the cheekbones with a mixture of L Nos 8 and 16 (Deep Brown)
Right Centre Create the impression of a longer nose by shading with L No. 16 on both sides at the top of the bridge

Below far left Highlight the top of the nose and the cheekbones with L No. 5
Below left The tone and colour of L No. 7 complements the Olive base to make a warm, soft eyeshadow
Above Draw in lower eyelines with the black pencil, lifting them at the outer corners. No eyelines have been used on the top lids; notice the difference this makes

Above The richness of L Carmine 3 makes it the most suitable lip colour. Make up the neck with Aquacolour – any unmadeup exposed skin will make nonsense of all your efforts – and this warning of course applies to hands too. Now douse your work in translucent powder and brush away the surplus

Left Finally, reinforce your eyebrows with your pencil

A Pantomime Dame

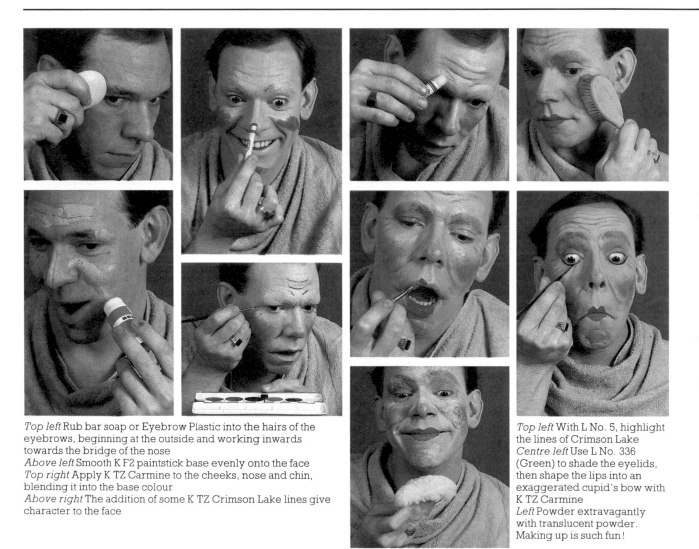

Top left Rub bar soap or Eyebrow Plastic into the hairs of the eyebrows, beginning at the outside and working inwards towards the bridge of the nose
Above left Smooth K F2 paintstick base evenly onto the face
Top right Apply K TZ Carmine to the cheeks, nose and chin, blending it into the base colour
Above right The addition of some K TZ Crimson Lake lines give character to the face

Top left With L No. 5, highlight the lines of Crimson Lake
Centre left Use L No. 336 (Green) to shade the eyelids, then shape the lips into an exaggerated cupid's bow with K TZ Carmine
Left Powder extravagantly with translucent powder. Making up is such fun!

Left Brush off excess powder with a soft brush
Below left Eyelines should be very heavy, so draw them in with K TZ Black on a No. 2 brush, *after* powdering

Above With the black pencil, draw in wildly exaggerated eyebrows, and fake eyelashes
Right The Pantomime Dame, wig firmly in place, is now ready for anything

Pantomime Dames wear at least two wigs during a performance. For most of the time, they wear a ''working wig'' like the one on the previous page. But for the grand finale, the Dame will make her entrance in a spectacular 'walkdown wig''

A Cast of Characters

In this glossary are listed some of the most popular plays and musicals performed on the British amateur stage at the beginning of the 1980s. The principal players of each production are given and their personalities briefly analysed. These analyses are keyed to those pages of this book upon which you will find the relevant characteristics portrayed in makeup. Of course, your Director or Producer may well have a different conception of the part he wishes you to play, in which case you must find the appropriate references in the Character and Personality Traits sections on pages 27–59.

The ages of the characters are included in the list that follows and, depending upon your own age, you will need to refer to the descriptions of the Straight, the Ageing and the Rejuvenating makeups on pages 22–25, 30–31 and 32–33 respectively. Sometimes, you will need to combine two or more aspects of these makeups to achieve the personality of the character you are portraying.

Play/Author Setting/Period	Principal Characters	Age and Characteristics
A Christmas Carol Charles Dickens adapted by Shaun Sutton London, 1870s	Ebeneezer Scrooge Bob Cratchit Marley's Ghost Mr Fezziwig Tiny Tim	old, misanthropic (page 52) 40s, thin (pages 34–35), kindly (page 56) old, ghostly, gloomy (page 57) 50–60, jolly (page 56) 8, a cripple, pale and ill-looking (pages 42–43)
A Doll's House Henrik Ibsen	Torvald Helmer Nora Helmer Nils Krogstad	38, domineering (page 54) 30, beautiful (pages 22–26), childlike and naïve (page 53) 40, embittered (page 52)
A Man for all Seasons Robert Bolt England, sixteenth century	Sir Thomas More Margaret More Lady Alice More Henry VIII Wolsey Thomas Cromwell Thomas Cranmer The Common Man	48, straight (pages 22–26) 24, beautiful (pages 22–26) clever (page 49), good (page 56) 47, straight (pages 22–26) 30, handsome (pages 22–26) 65, dominating (page 54) 38, subtle (page 52) 48, cunning (page 52), ruthless (page 54) middle-aged, crafty (page 52), kindly (page 56)

Play/Author Setting/Period	Principal Characters	Age and Characteristics
A Midsummer Night's Dream William Shakespeare Athens, and a wood near it	Oberon	handsome (pages 22–26), a fairy king (pages 70–71)
	Titania	beautiful (pages 22–26), a fairy queen (pages 70–71)
	Puck	an imp (pages 70–71)
	Hermia	young, beautiful, Greek (pages 76–77 and page 26)
	Helena	young, pretty, Greek (pages76–77 and page 26)
	Lysander	young, handsome, Greek (pages 76–77 and page 26)
	Demetrius	young, handsome, Greek (pages 76–77 and (page 26)
	Bottom, a weaver	simple (page 51), moon-faced (page 53)
A Voyage Round My Father John Mortimer	Father	60s, blind, eccentric and difficult (page 50)
	Mother	50s, motherly and affectionate (page 56)
	Son	30s, conventional (page 51)
An Inspector Calls J. B. Priestley England, 1912	Arthur Birling	50s, heavy-looking (pages 36–37), portentous (page 58)
	Gerald Croft	30, attractive (pages 22–26), well-bred (page 49)
	Eric Birling	25, uncertain (page 53)
	Inspector Gode	50, solid (pages 36–37), purposeful (page 54)
	Sheila Birling	20s, pretty (pages 22–26)
	Sybil Birling	50, cold (page 54)
And a Nightingale Sang C. P. Taylor Newcastle, 1939–1945	Helen Stott	early 30s, plain (page 51), gradually puts on more makeup during play
	Norman	early 30s, attractive rather than handsome (pages 22–26)
	Joyce Stott	early 20s, very pretty (pages 22–26)
	Eric	early 20s, handsome (pages 22–26)
	George Stott	50s, miner, shows signs of hard working life, straight (pages 22–26)
	Peggy Stott	50s, straight (pages 22–26)
	Andie	70s, straight (pages 22–26)
Abigail's Party Mike Leigh Suburbia, present day	Beverly	30s, empty-headed (page 53), assertive (page 54), without taste (page 59)
	Laurence	30s, aggressive (page 54), tense and touchy (page 57)
	Angela	30s, plain (page 51)

Play/Author Setting/Period	Principal Characters	Age and Characteristics
Abigail's Party	Tony	30s, ordinary (page 51), robust, red-haired
	Susan	40s, lonely, strained and worried (page 57)
Absurd Person Singular Alan Ayckbourn England, 1970s	Jane Hopcraft	30s, helpful and nice (page 56), naïve (page 53), without taste (page 59)
	Sidney Hopcraft	30s, cheery and easy-going (page 56)
	Ronald Brewster	mid-40s, impressive (page 54)
	Marion Brewster	early 40s, well-groomed and well-preserved (page 49), very snobbish (page 58)
	Eva Jackson	30s, well-dressed (page 49), depressive in Act 2 (page 57)
	Geoffrey Jackson	mid-30s, good-looking (pages 22–26) easy-going (page 56)
Bedroom Farce Alan Ayckbourn England, 1970s	Ernest	nearly 60, forgetful (page 50)
	Delia	late 50s, pleasant and helpful (page 56)
	Nick	young, suffering and full of self-pity (page 57)
	Jan	young, commonsensical (page 51), jolly (page 56)
	Malcolm	young, excitable (page 50), sociable (page 56)
	Kate	young, amiable and patient (page 56)
	Trevor	young, temperamental (page 50), self-torturing (page 57)
Billy Liar Keith Waterhouse and Willis Hall An industrial town in the north of England, 1960	Billy Fisher	19, slightly built (pages 34–35), day-dreamer (page 53)
	Geoffrey Fisher	early 50s, coarse (page 48), dominating (page 54)
	Alice Fisher	mid-40s, straight (pages 22–26)
	Rita	17, blonde, common, tarty and hard (page 59)
	Barbara	19, large and well-built (pages 36–37), conventional (page 51)
	Florence Boothroyd	80s, forgetful (page 50)
Blithe Spirit Noël Coward England, 1941	Ruth	35, smart and organized (page 49), determined (page 54), attractive (pages 22–26)
	Elvira	young, beautiful (pages 22–26, can use K No. 1742 which is based on the special makeup devised for the part)

Play/Author Setting/Period	**Principal Characters**	Age and Characteristics
Blithe Spirit	Charles	40, personable (page 56), good-looking (pages 22–26), stylish (page 49)
	Madame Arcati	45 +, eccentric and dotty (page 50), spinsterish (page 55), flamboyant (page 59) *(Ruth and Elvira should look physically very similar)*
Born in the Gardens Peter Nichols Bristol, present day	Maud	70, going senile (page 50), favours Second World War makeup
	Hedley	50, good-looking (pages 22–26), full smile (page 56), worried (page 57)
	Queenie	45, deep tan, looks 35, sophisticated and well-dressed (page 49)
	Mo	45, looks all of his age and more, glasses, neat and boring (page 51) *(Queenie and Mo are twins)*
The Boyfriend Sandy Wilson Villa Caprice, near Nice, 1926	Polly Brown Tony	18, pretty (pages 22–26) young, shy (page 53), handsome (pages 22–26)
	Madame Dubbonet	middle-aged, attractive femme fatale (pages 22–26), eccentric (page 50)
	Percival Browne	40, honest (page 53), paternalistic (page 56)
	Lord Brockhurst Maisie Bobby van Husen	60s, sex-mad eccentric (page 50) 18, very pretty (pages 22–26) 20s, handsome (pages 22–26), excitable (page 50)
	Hortense	20–30, attractive (pages 22–26)
Cabaret lyrics by Fred Ebb, music by John Kander Berlin, early 1930s	Sally Bowles Clifford Bradshaw	20s, decadent and outrageous (page 59 20s, naïve (page 53), handsome (pages 22–26)
	the MC	ageless, subtle (page 52), sophisticated (page 49)
		(Find reference for the decadent cabaret makeup of the period)

Play/Author Setting/Period	Principal Characters	Age and Characteristics
Carousel lyrics by Oscar Hammerstein II, music by Richard Rodgers New England, 1983	Billy Bigelow Julie Jordan Louise	straight (pages 22–26) middle-aged, innocent (page 53) young, straight (pages 22–26)
Charley's Aunt Brandon Thomas Oxford, 1882	Jack Chesney Charles Wykeham Lord Fancourt Babberley Donna Lucia d'Alvadorex Amy Spettigue Kitty Verdun	22, tall, dark and good-looking (pages 22–26) 20, fair, good-looking (pages 22–26), shy (page 53) young, small, good-looking (pages 22–26), cheerful (page 56), plays in drag for much of the play middle-aged, beautiful (pages 22–26), kindly and cheerful (page 56) young, pretty (pages 22–26) young, pretty (pages 22–26)
Chicago lyrics by Fred Ebb, music by John Kander Chicago, 1930s	Roxie Hart Velma Kelly Billy Flynn Amost Hart Wardress (Mama) Morton	30s, attractive (pages 22–26), has style (page 49) 30s, quite attractive (pages 22–26) 30s, flamboyant (page 59), successful (page 49) 40s, insignificant (page 51) hard, tough and repressive (page 54)
The Dresser Ronald Harwood English provinces, 1942	Norman Sir	middle-aged, fussy (page 55) elderly, going senile (page 50)
Fiddler on the Roof lyrics by Sheldon Harnic, music by Jerry Bock Anatevka, Russia, 1905	Tevye, the Milkman Golde, his wife Motel, the Tailor Tzeitel Lazar Wolfe, the Butcher	middle-aged, quite severe (page 54), paternalistic and kindly (page 56) middle-aged, determined (page 54), motherly (page 56) 20s, shy and reserved (page 53), quietly determined (page 54) 19, quite attractive (pages 22–26), shy (page 53) middle-aged, fat (pages 36–37), slightly pompous (page 58)

Play/Author Setting/Period	Principal Characters	Age and Characteristics
Fiddler on the Roof	**Yente, the Matchmaker**	70s, fussy and interfering (page 55)
	Fruma-Sarah	green spirit come back to haunt (pages 70–71), domineering (page 54)
Gaslight Patrick Hamilton Victorian England	**Jack Manningham**	45, tall, good-looking (pages 22–26), sinister (page 52)
	Bella Manningham	34, once lovely (pages 22–26), haggard and ill-looking (page 57)
	ex-Detective Rough	over 60, greying (pages 30–31), short and wiry
	Elizabeth	50, stout (pages 36–37), amiable (page 56)
	Nancy	19, pretty (pages 22–26)
Gigi Colette and Anita Loos Paris, 1900	**Gigi**	16, gawky and tomboyish, enchanting (pages 22–26)
	Gaston Lachaille (Tonton)	30, handsome (pages 22–26), smart (page 49)
	Great Aunt Alicia	70, frail-looking (pages 42–43) but business-like
	Madame Alvarez	60, imposing (page 54)
	Andrée	32, faded (pages 42–43), discouraged (page 57)
	Sidonie	young, happy (page 56)
	Victor	elderly, charming (pages 22–26)
The Gondoliers lyrics by William Gilbert, music by Arthur Sullivan Venice, about 1750	**The Duke of Plaza-Toro**	50, strong and determined (page 54) but fair, Italian (pages 76–77)
	The Duchess of Plaza-Toro	40s, elegant and assured (page 49), Italian (pages 76–77)
	Luiz	20s, handsome, Italian (pages 76–77 and page 26)
	Casilda	21, very pretty, Italian (pages 76–77 and page 26)
	Marco Palmieri	20s, handsome, Italian (pages 76–77) and page 26)
	Guiseppe Palmieri	20s, handsome, Italian (pages 76–77 and page 26)
	Don Alhambra del Bolero	40s, dressed in black, solemn and stern (page 54), Italian (pages 76–77)
Guys and Dolls lyrics and music by Frank Loesser New York, 1930s	**Miss Sarah Brown**	20s, sweet and very attractive (pages 22–26), but should not look as if wearing makeup
	Sky Masterson	30s, handsome (pages 22–26)
	Nathan Detroit	40s, smart, (page 49)
	Miss Adelaide	late 30s, attractive (pages 22–36), has permanent cold

Play/Author Setting/Period	Principal Characters	Age and Characteristics
Habeas Corpus Alan Bennett Hove, Sussex present day	Arthur Wicksteed	50s, smart (page 49)
	Muriel Wicksteed	middle-aged, voluptuous, attractive (pages 22–26)
	Constance Wicksteed	middle-aged, no bust, spinsterish (page 55)
	Denis Wicksteed	early 20s, hypochondriac so looks ill (page 57)
	Lady Rumper	early middle-age, slightly shabby, sophisticated (page 49)
	Felicity Rumper	20s, a sex symbol, very attractive (pages 22–26)
	Sir Percy Shorter	middle-aged, loud and pompous (page 58), aggressive (page 54)
	Canon Throbbing	early middle-age, sex-starved (page 55), twittish (page 50)
	Mr Shanks	early middle-age, quiet (page 53)
	Mrs Swabb	middle-aged, cleaning-lady type, often played by a man (pages 78–80)
	Mr Purdue	any age, manic depressive (page 57)
Half a Sixpence Beverley Cross lyrics and music by David Heneker England 1900	Arthur Kipps	young, open-faced and honest (page 53), personable (page 56)
	Ann Pornick	young, pretty (pages 22–26), pleasant (page 56)
	Helen Walsingham	young, beautiful (pages 22–26)
Hamlet William Shakespeare Elsinore	Hamlet	young, handsome (pages 22–26)
	Claudius	middle-aged, apparently pleasant (page 56), but evil (page 52)
	Horatio	young, handsome (pages 22–26)
	Polonius	50s, a busy-body (page 55)
	Laertes	young, naïve (page 53)
	Gertrude	40s, straight (pages 22–26)
	Ophelia	young, beautiful (pages 22–26), innocent (page 53)
Hello Dolly lyrics and music by Jerry Herman	Dolly Gallagher Levi	40s, attractive (pages 22–26), flamboyant (page 59)
	Horace Vandergelder	40s–50s, quite good-looking (pages 22–26)
	Ermengarde	20s, attractive (pages 22–26)
	Ambrose	20s, handsome (pages 22–26)
	Ernestine Money	young, very fat (pages 36–37)

Play/Author Setting/Period	Principal Characters	Age and Characteristics
Hobson's Choice Harold Brighouse Salford, Lancashire, 1880	**Henry Horatio Hobson**	55, florid (page 48), stubborn (page 54)
	Maggie Hobson	30, efficient and organized (page 49)
	William Mossop (Willie)	30, contented and unambitious (page 56)
	Alice Hobson	23, quite pretty (pages 22–26)
	Vicky Hobson	21, very pretty (pages 22–26)
	Albert Prosser	26, well-dressed (page 49)
	Fred Beenstock	young, attractive (pages 22–26)
The Importance of Being Earnest Oscar Wilde England, 1890s	**Algernon Moncrief**	young, elegant (page 49)
	John Worthing	young, elegant (page 49)
	Lady Bracknell	middle-aged or elderly, formidable and determined (page 54)
	Hon. Gwendolen Fairfax	young, handsome (pages 22–26)
	Cecily Cardew	young, lovely (pages 22–26)
	Miss Prism	middle-aged, spinsterish (page 55)
Joking Apart Alan Ayckbourn England, 1970s	**Richard**	late 20s, charming (pages 22–26), self-assured (page 49), sociable (page 56)
	Anthea	mid-20s, cheerful (page 56), frank (page 53)
	Hugh	26, shy and nervous (page 53), quietly determined (page 54)
	Louise	24, on drugs therefore pale and tense (page 57)
	Sven	30 trying to be 50, self-important and ponderous (page 58)
	Olive	28, staid (page 58)
	Melody	young, brash (page 58)
	Mandy	young, quiet (page 53)
	Mo	young, excitable (page 50)
	Debbie	young, pleasant (page 56)
The King and I lyrics by Oscar Hammerstein II music by Richard Rodgers Bangkok	**Anna Leonowens**	30s, beautiful (pages 22–26), sophisticated (page 49)
	The King of Siam	50s, handsome (pages 22–26), stubborn (page 54)
	Louis	teenager, straight (pages 22–26)
	Tuptim	young, very beautiful (pages 22–26)
	Lun Tha	handsome (pages 22–26) but impoverished

Play/Author Setting/Period	Principal Characters	Age and Characteristics
The Last of the Red Hot Lovers Neil Simon An Apartment, present day	Barney Cashman Elaine Navazio Bobbi Michele Jeanette Fisher	47, gentle (page 56), neat (page 51) late 30s, modestly dressed, attractive (pages 22–26) about 27, pretty (pages 22–26), cool (page 49) about 39, totally depressed and gloomy (page 57), nervous (page 53)
The Lion in Winter James Goldman Henry's castle at Chinon	Henry II Richard Geoffrey John Philip Cadet Eleanor Alais	50, handsome (pages 22–26) 26, tall, graceful, impressive (page 54) 25, slim, darkly attractive (pages 22–26) 16, short, pudgy (pages 36–37), with pimples and a sweet smile (page 56) 17, handsome (pages 22–26), direct (page 53) 61, handsome (pages 22–26), assured (page 49), does not look her age 23, serenely beautiful (pages 22–26), innocent (page 53)
The Merchant of Venice William Shakespeare Venice and Belmont on the Continent	Antonio Bassanio Lorenzo Shylock Portia Nerissa Jessica	30s, handsome, Italian (pages 76–77 and page 26) 30s, good-looking, Italian (pages 76–77 and page 26) 20s, good-looking, Italian (pages 76–77 and page 26) 45+, hard and mean, Jewish (page 52 and page 65) early 30s, beautiful, Italian (pages 76–77 and page 26) young, pretty, Italian (pages 76–77 and page 26) young, beautiful, Jewish (pages 76–77, page 26 and page 65)
The Merry Widow lyrics by Adrian Ross music by Franz Lehár Marsovian Embassy, Paris	Sonia Sadoya Prince Danilo Baron Popoff Natalia Popoff Camille de Jolidon	young, beautiful (pages 22–26) young, dashing and handsome (pages 22–26) 50, fussy (page 55) 30s, beautiful (pages 22–26) young, handsome (pages 22–26)

Play/Author Setting/Period	Principal Characters	Age and Characteristics
The Mikado lyrics by William Gilbert, music by Arthur Sullivan The Town of Titipu, Japan	The Mikado	50s, Japanese (pages 72–73) stern (page 54)
	Nanki-Poo	young, handsome, Japanese (pages 72–73 and page 26)
	Ko-Ko, Lord High Executioner	middle-aged, a flirt, Japanese (pages 72–73)
	Poo-Bah, Lord High Everything Else	middle-aged, Japanese (pages 72–73), pompous (page 58), powerful (page 54)
	Yum-Yum	young, very pretty, Japanese (pages 72–73 and page 26)
	Katisha	middle-aged, Japanese (pages 72–73), plain (page 51)
Much Ado About Nothing William Shakespeare Messina	Don Pedro	40s, Italian (pages 76–77), authoritative (page 54), sympathetic (page 56)
	Don John	40s, Italian (pages 76–77), evil (page 52)
	Claudio	30, handsome, Italian (pages 76–77 and page 26)
	Benedick	30s, good-looking, Italian (pages 76–77 and page 26), domineering (page 54)
	Hero	20s, beautiful, Italian (pages 76–77 and page 26)
	Beatrice	20s, handsome, Italian (pages 76–77 and page 26)
	Dogberry	Italian (pages 76–77), simple (page 51)
Murder at the Vicarage Agatha Christie, dramatized by Moie Charles and Barbara Toy England, 1930s	Miss Marple	middle-aged, neat (page 51), eccentric (page 50)
	Anne Protheroe	35, very attractive (pages 22–26)
	Lawrence Redding	30, charming (pages 22–26), ruthless (page 54)
	Reverend Leonard Clement	40s, charming (pages 22–26), vague (page 50)
	Inspector Slack	middle-aged, small, energetic, ordinary (page 51)
	Mrs Price Ridley	middle-aged, severe (page 54)
	Dennis	16, straight (pages 22–26)
	Ronald Hawes	young, pale (pages 42–43), nervous (page 53)
	Dr Haydock	elderly, straight (pages 22–26)
	Mrs Clement	young, pretty (pages 22–26)
	Lettice Protheroe	17, slight (pages 34–35)

Play/Author Setting/Period	Principal Characters	Age and Characteristics
My Three Angels Sam and Bella Spewack Prison colony of Cayenne, 1890s	**Felix Dulay**	middle-aged, kindly (page 56)
	Emilie Dulay	middle-aged, attractive (pages 22–26), motherly (page 56)
	Marie-Louise Dulay	20s, pretty (pages 22–26)
	Alfred	20s, handsome (pages 22–26)
	Jules	40s, assured (page 49)
	Joseph	40s, efficient and organized (page 49)
	Gaston Lemare	middle-aged, pompous and a bully (page 58)
	Paul Cassagon	20s, good-looking (pages 22–26), weak (page 53)
Oklahoma! lyrics by Oscar Hammerstein II, music by Richard Rodgers Indian Territory, 1900	**Curly McLain**	young, good-looking (pages 22–26)
	Laurey Williams	young, pretty (pages 22–26)
	Aunt Eller Murphy	middle-aged, straight (pages 22–26)
	Jud Fry	young, gloomy (page 57)
Oliver lyrics and music by Lionel Bart North of England and London, 1850	**Oliver**	a boy, innocent and fresh-faced (page 53)
	Mr Bumble	middle-aged, pompous (page 58)
	Fagin	45 + , bearded (pages 60–63), ill-looking (pages 42–43), Jewish (page 65)
	Nancy	late 20s, pretty (pages 22–26), motherly (page 56)
	Bill Sykes	late 30s, mean and nasty (page 52)
	The Artful Dodger	15–16, happy (page 40–41), cunning (page 52)
Once a Catholic Mary O'Malley Harlesdon, 1956–7	**Mother Peter**	60s, ordinary (page 51)
	Mary Mooney	15, open-faced and naive (page 53)
	Mary Gallagher	15, clever (page 49)
	Mary McGinty	15, attractive (pages 22–26), tarty (page 59)
	Derek	17, a Teddy boy, ordinary (page 51)
	Cuthbert	17, spotty, naive (page 53)

A CAST OF CHARACTERS

Play/Author Setting/Period	Principal Characters	Age and Characteristics
One Flew Over the Cuckoo's Nest Dale Wasserman England, a mental hospital, present day	Nurse Ratched	about 40, handsome (pages 22–26), hard and tough (page 54)
	Billy	30, childlike (page 53)
	Dr Spivey	30s or 40s, ordinary (page 51), harassed (page 57)
	Cheswick	short, chubby (pages 36–37)
	Martini	Italian (pages 76–77), excitable (page 50)
	Ruckly	blank-faced (page 51)
Patience lyrics by William Gilbert, music by Arthur Sullivan Castle Bunthorne and a glade	Colonel Calverley	whiskered (pages 60–63)
	Major Murgatroyd	whiskered (pages 60–63)
	Lt. the Duke of Dunstable	young, to begin with in low spirits (page 87), good-looking (pages 22–26)
	The Lady Saphir	young, beautiful (pages 22–26)
	The Lady Angela	young beautiful (pages 22–26)
	The Lady Jane	young, beautiful (pages 22–26)
	Reginald Bunthorne	young, handsome (pages 22–26), affected (page 50)
	Archibald Grosvenor	young, beautiful (pages 22–26)
	Patience	young, pretty (pages 22–26), happy (page 56)
The Pirates of Penzance lyrics by William Gilbert, music by Arthur Sullivan A rocky seashore on the coast of Cornwall	Major-General Stanley	60s, slightly pompous (page 58), paternal (page 56)
	The Pirate King	30s, handsome (pages 22–26)
	Frederic	21, very handsome (pages 22–26)
	Ruth	40s, plain (page 51)
	Mabel	20, very pretty (pages 22–26)
Present Laugher Noël Coward London, 1938	Garry Essendine	30s, handsome (pages 22–26), arrogant (page 58), sophisticated and self-assured (page 49)
	Liz Essendine	30s, charming (pages 22–26), stylish (page 49)
	Roland Maule	young, uncertain (page 53)
	Johanna Lyppiatt	30s, exquisite (page 22–26), assured (page 49)
	Monica Reed	40s, pleasant (page 56), austere and strong-minded (page 54)
	Miss Erikson	into spiritualism, dotty (page 50)

Play/Author Setting/Period	Principal Characters	Age and Characteristics
Princess Ida lyrics by William Gilbert, music by Arthur Sullivan King Hildebrand's Palace and Castle Adamant	King Hildebrand Hilarion King Gama Princess Ida Lady Blanche	50s, kindly (page 56) 22, handsome (pages 22–26) 50, ugly and misshapen (page 48), unhappy (pages 38–39) 21, beautiful (pages 22–26), determined (page 54) 20s, handsome (pages 22–26), ambitious (page 49)
Pygmalion George Bernard Shaw London, 1914	Eliza Doolittle Henry Higgins Colonel Pickering	early 20s, attractive (pages 22–26), self-sufficient (page 49) 40s, handsome (pages 22–26), arrogant (page 54), eccentric (page 50) 60s, whiskered (pages 60–63), kindly (page 56)
Rebecca Daphne de Maurier Cornwall, 1940	Mrs de Winter Maxim de Winter Mrs Danvers	very young, pretty (pages 22–26), naive and shy (page 53) 35–45), handsome (pages 22–26), experienced and sophisticated (page 49) 40–50), austere (page 54), mysterious (page 52), dressed in black
Semi-Detached David Turner Dowlihull, 1960s	Fred Medway Hilda Medway Tom Medway Eileen Medway Avril Hadfield	50, conventional (page 51) 48, conventional (page 51) 19, pleasant (page 56) 20, attractive (pages 22–26) but sensible 22, smart (page 49) but cheap
The Servant Robin Maugham Chelsea, London, 1970s	Richard Merton Sally Grant Tony Williams Barrett Vera Mabel	about 30, lean (pages 34–35), pleasant (page 56) 25, pretty (pages 22–26), fresh-faced (page 53) about 30, tanned (pages 76–77), well-built (pages 36–37) 30–50, quiet (page 53), appears ordinary (page 51) 17, slender (pages 34–35), pale (pages 42–43) young, slim and small, pretty (pages 22–26)

Play/Author Setting/Period	Principal Characters	Age and Characteristics
She Stoops to Conquer Oliver Goldsmith Eighteenth century England	**Tony Lumpkin**	21, simple (page 51)
	Marlow	young, handsome (pages 22–26), shy (page 53)
	Hastings	young, handsome (pages 22–26)
	Kate Hardcastle	young, lovely (pages 22–26)
	Constance Neville	20, pretty (pages 22–26)
	Mr Hardcastle	60s, amiable (page 56)
	Mrs Hardcastle	57, affected (page 50)
Spring and Port Wine Bill Naughton Bolton, 1970	**Daisy Crompton**	47, placid and seemingly contented (page 56)
	Rafe Crompton	50, solid and confident (page 54), paternalistic (page 56), stubborn (page 58)
	Hilda Crompton	19, pretty (pages 22–26)
	Wilfred Crompton	18, looks younger, fresh-faced and nervous (page 53), likeable (page 56)
	Harold Crompton	23, good-looking (pages 22–26)
	Florence Crompton	25, brisk and self-assured (page 49)
Sweeney Todd Christopher Bond London, early nineteenth century	**Sweeney Todd**	middle-aged, bitter and hard (page 52)
	Mrs Lovett	middle-aged, stoutish (pages 36–37), slightly vulgar (page 48)
	Anthony Hope	young, handsome (pages 22–26)
	Johanna	young, pretty (pages 22–26), gentle (page 56)
	Tobias Ragg	young, not very bright (page 53)
	Judge Turpin	elderly, lascivious (page 48)
	The Beggar Woman	apparently elderly and grey-haired (pages 30–31)
Ten Times Table Alan Ayckbourn The Swan Hotel Ballroom, England 1970s	**Ray**	40s, pleasant (page 56)
	Donald	50s, grey (pages 30–31), serious, fussy (pages 54–55)
	Helen	about 40, handsome (pages 22–26), smart and classy (page 49)
	Sophie	early 30s, fresh-faced (page 53)
	Eric	young, bearded (pages 60–63)
	Audrey	old, permanently smiling (page 56)
	Lawrence	40s, florid (page 48), tense (page 57)
	Tim	40s, organizing (page 49)
	Philippa	young, amiable (page 56), very shy (page 53)
	Max Kirkov	young, powerful (page 54), black-haired

Play/Author Setting/Period	Principal Characters	Age and Characteristics
Twelfth Night William Shakespeare Illyria	**Orsino, Duke of Illyria**	30s, austere (page 54), sympathetic (page 56)
	Sebastian	20s, handsome (pages 22–26)
	Sir Toby Belch	middle-aged, short and fat (pages 36–37), dissipated (page 48)
	Sir Andrew Aguecheek	young, tall and thin (pages 34–35), dissipated (page 48)
	Malvolio	40s, dresses in black, very depressed (page 57), pompous (page 58)
	Olivia	20s, beautiful (pages 22–26)
	Viola	20s, beautiful (pages 22–26) (*Viola and Sebastian are twins*)
The Wizard of Oz lyrics by Noël Langley, music by Florence Ryerson and Edgar Allen Woolf Kansas and the Land of Oz	**Dorothy Gale**	12–14, young, innocent (page 53)
	Cowardly Lion	scared-looking (page 57)
	Tin Man	worried-looking (page 57)
	Scarecrow	silly-looking (page 50)
	Wicked Witch of the West	evil (page 52)
	Glinda, the Good Witch	kind and motherly (page 56)
	The Wonderful Wizard	ordinary and small with glasses (page 51), quite stout (pages 36–37)
The Winslow Boy Terence Rattigan	**Arthur Winslow**	60, domineering and stubborn (page 54)
	Ronnie Winslow	14, straight (pages 22–26)
	Catherine Winslow	30, mannish (page 55)
	Grace Winslow	50, faded and pretty (pages 22–26)
	Dickie Winslow	20, large (pages 36–37), cheerful (page 56)
	Sir Robert Morton	early 40s, elegant (page 49), cadaverous (pages 34–35)
The Yeoman of the Guard lyrics by William Gilbert, music by Arthur Sullivan Tower of London, sixteenth century	**Colonel Fairfax**	young, handsome (pages 22–26)
	Sergeant Meryll	middle-aged, paternalistic (page 56)
	Jack Point	a fool, appears simple (page 51)
	Wilfred Shadbolt	young, lovesick and depressed (page 57)
	Elsie Maynard	young, pretty (pages 22–26)
	Phoebe Meryll	young, pretty (pages 22–26)
	Dame Carruthers	elderly, grey (pages 30–31), proud and determined (page 54)

Index

Bibliography and Reference

The Art of Stage Lighting
   Frederick Bentham, 3rd Edition, Pitman House 1980
Contacts No. 73, The Spotlight 1983–84
The Guide to Selecting Plays Part 1, Samuel French Ltd 1983–84
Gold and Silver Bernard Grun, W. H. Allen 1970
The Handbook of Gilbert and Sullivan
   compiled by Frank Ledlie Moore, Arthur Barker 1972
The Hollywood Musical Clive Hirschhorn, Octopus 1981
The Illustrated Encyclopedia of World Theatre, Thames and Hudson 1977
Stage Makeup Herman Buchman, Pitman Publishing 1974
Stage Makeup Richard Corson, sixth edition, Prentice-Hall 1981
They're Playing Our Song Max Wilk, W. H. Allen 1974

Acknowledgements

Michael Cyprien and Bert Broe would like to thank those good and patient friends whose changing faces grace the pages of this book. John McHugh, Cathy Taplin, Julie Dartnell, Ivor Williams, Jane Broe, Vanessa Hibbert, Pamela Goodchild, Joan Marsh, Julia Ladds, Stephen Reynolds, Deborah Manship, Stanley Taplin, David Emerson, Louise Cyprien, Hilary Field, Janine Stewart, Carl Williams, and of course Roy Dotrice for his support and encouragement.

Spectator Publications are also indebted to Vanessa Furse, Stephen Reynolds and Tana Russell for their professional help and advice in the compilation of the Cast of Characters.

And finally, to Simon (Wigs) Limited, 2 New Burlington Street, London W1, go thanks for the loan of Mr Dotrice's King Lear wig, and to Morris Angel and Son Limited, 119 Shaftesbury Avenue, London WC2 for the loan of his costume.